D0230236

LONDON BOROUGH OF GREENWICH

GREENWICH LIBRARIES

RESERVE STOCK (P)

LSZ0016

GREENWICH LIBRARIES

3 8028 00855753 7

2. 2.

World
Soccer Skills

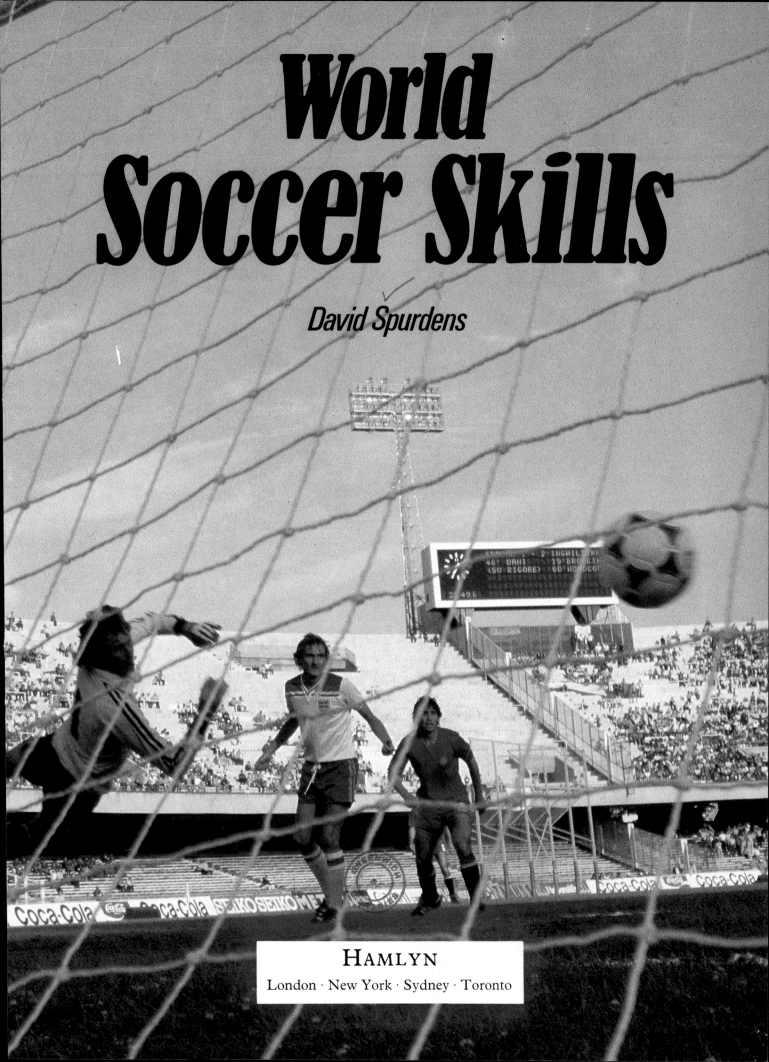

World Soccer Skills

David Spurdens

HAMLYN

London · New York · Sydney · Toronto

SBN 1   2   3   LOC. COPY

600 38552 3 2

EDITION
DATE   1984

CLASS
NO.   796.3342

INVOICE JM   20 JUN 1985 £595

Ray Wilkins in Manchester United colours.

Contents

First published in 1984 by
The Hamlyn Publishing Group Limited
London · New York · Sydney · Toronto
Astronaut House, Feltham, Middlesex, England

© Copyright The Hamlyn Publishing Group Limited 1984

All rights reserved. No part of this publication may be
reproduced, stored in a retrieval system, or transmitted, in
any form or by any means, electronic, mechanical, photocopying,
or otherwise without the permission of The Hamlyn Publishing
Group Limited.

ISBN 0 600 38552 3

Printed in Spain

Cover : Colour photographs by Associated Sports Photography
(George Herringshaw)
Black and white photographs by David Spurdens

The ultimate in a player's career. Dino Zoff, the Italian captain, holds aloft the World Cup won by his country in Spain in 1982.

Introduction

Football, like most things, has fallen prey to the needs of the materialist society. Success is measured in terms of the balance sheet and the trophy cupboard. Managers and coaches, even at the professional level, would like to mould teams to play the game they love as it should be played, with skill, verve and enjoyment. But economic pressures and the demands of a largely parochial public who want to see their team win at all costs, have bred a cautious attitude. Managers and coaches have found that to keep their jobs, freedom of expression must be tempered with a safety-first attitude. 'Give nothing away' is the first order of the day – the fancy bits can come later.

This attitude, while it affects soccer all round the world, is most found in Britain, perhaps because in the 92 clubs of the Football League, plus those of the Scottish League, Britain possesses more strength in depth than any other nation. A bad run of a few seasons, such as happened to Blackpool and Sheffield United in the 1970s, can see a team drop through the divisions and change from one of soccer's aristocrats to a 'has-been'. The pressure to succeed increases the penalties for failure.

Not everybody has succumbed to this trend however. Over the same few years some South American and European teams have played exciting, creative and successful football. They have proved that players with individual skill can triumph over teams of a more functional nature.

It is hoped that this book will stimulate a recognition of the value of individuality, and reawaken our love of individual skills. Perhaps we should say confirm our love of individual play, because it has always been the great individualists, the stars of the calibre of Stanley Matthews, Puskas, Pelé, Beckenbauer, Cruyff, Best and Rummenigge, who have drawn the crowds and become legends.

The Continentals and South Americans have not been fully converted to the sophistication of modern coaching developments, and have remained truer to the natural learning situation which goes with a back alley and a tennis ball. Young players in England have come too soon under the influence of the patterns of English league football. Consequently the range of things they can do with a ball in any given situation is limited. It is to fill this void, and to attempt to develop a positive new attitude towards ball mastery, that this book is written. No player will be able to add all the skills in this book to his repertoire. But he can master some, and in so much football the moments of pure skill are rare tasty morsels in a stodgy staple diet. The player who performs them is remembered as the one who made an ordinary dish memorable.

In all walks of life, the more knowledge and skill a person has the more he will be able to cope satisfactorily with any given situation. In a sport such as soccer this is doubly true, because the game is so competitive and events occur so swiftly that a player had to choose his options in a flash. He reacts rather than considers. His skills must be instinctive. Only by learning and practising a skill so that it becomes as natural as walking will he be able to cope with the demands of a match.

In years of coaching I have come to realize there is a gulf between what a player *thinks* makes up a skill and what actually takes place. The first skill in this book, the Step Over, as performed by the great Brazilian forward Eder, was the subject of an experiment I conducted with three separate groups of boys, aged 10-12, 12-14 and 14-17. I demonstrated the Step Over and asked them to reproduce it. Nobody managed to do it properly. With each round of failure I demonstrated the skill again at a realistic speed. After six demonstrations I broke the skill down into parts, as in this book, and eventually everybody in the group began to reproduce the skill at a reasonable level.

This experiment demonstrates the need for a specific programme which separates the various mechanical stages of a skill.

Coaches, managers and teachers might like to conduct their own experiments. I have found that if a row of skittles is put down at two-metre intervals for dribbling practice, the young player will weave through them using the inside of both feet. It has to be suggested to him that there are numerous surfaces and techniques which he could use, e.g. the inside and outside of one foot, the outsides of both feet, a sole roll, a toe roll, various combinations of these and so on. The same applies to other skill problems. Throw a high ball to a player and it is invariably trapped by using the inside instep surface or by bringing the sole down on top of the ball. Hit a long ball along the ground and it can be predicted that it will be controlled with the inside instep. The possible responses in each case are numerous, but the player must be shown them, and must be shown how to perform them by breaking them down into their separate mechanical parts in a step-by-step sequence.

It is hoped that this book will be useful to two sets of people: to coaches, managers and teachers, who can use it as a basis for programmes of skill instruction, and to young players themselves, who can use it as their own personal coach, showing them in easy-to-follow stages how to perform the skills of the great players.

There is one final reason for compiling this book which has nothing to do with utility or productivity. It is to do with enjoyment: the unashamed enjoyment which comes with playing with a ball and gradually mastering that awkward and troublesome sphere. This enjoyment is the essence of football, and despite what some managers say about 'closing it down' and 'snatching a point', this is really 'what it's all about'.

Dribbling Skills

Dribbling is the art of a player with the ball beating or going past another player. Despite the rationalization of the game at large, with the emphasis on defensive tactics, or more logically because of it, it remains the most thrilling and fulfilling aspect of the game.

Players who can dribble are at a premium. They are few and far between. Today, with the higher degree of organization in the game, the artist who can run at players and beat them stands out more than he ever did. Not only has the nature of his undertaking become more complex, it has become more valuable.

The excitement in dribbling stems from the incessant variety of techniques a player can use to achieve his aim. It is only the most skilful players who can dribble effectively and open up defences.

Players throughout the ages have always had a dribbling identity, a personal group of characteristics as distinguishable as the nose or the chin on their faces.

The movements of Stanley Matthews of England or George Best of Northern Ireland were as distinctive as the movements of Diego Maradona of Argentina or Juanito of Spain. Their individual, exclusive patterns of running, stopping and turning all integrated smoothly with a variety of techniques and feints to dupe opponents into committing errors of judgement.

Ironically, although the number of great dribblers may have diminished, the art of dribbling is a more familiar one to a wider variety of players. With 'total' football and the involvement of all players in a greater responsibility, every player in the team at some time or other calls upon the skill either to get out of trouble or to get into forward positions.

The full back or even central defender running with the ball and beating players is a familiar sight, whereas in bygone years such positions had a more functional responsibility accompanied by greater territorial restrictions.

Nowadays, in all aspects of football, the wider the range of techniques a player has at his disposal the more likely he is to be successful.

For techniques to be absorbed into a player's repertoire of skills they must be thoroughly learned, at first in practice situations without stress, so that the player grows to feel confident in their regular use in competitive games.

The foundation of all good dribbling techniques is the ability to run with the ball. At first, this seems a simple process which most players should master quite easily in the early days of their career. But this is not quite so. There is more to running with the ball than meets the eye.

The captain of Scotland, Graeme Souness, in possession of the ball while the captain of Brazil, Socrates, moves in to challenge, during the World Cup match in 1982.

1 Running with the ball using the 'inside foot' technique.

2 Running with the ball using the 'outside foot' technique.

3 The ball being moved forward using the insides of both feet, transferring the ball diagonally.

4 The ball travelling from foot to foot with the trunk swaying beyond the line of the controlling foot.

5 Playing on the right flank with the dribbler (a) dragging the ball inside with the right foot and (b) outside with the left foot.

6 Bringing the body across the ball, dummying the marker and bypassing him in the opposite direction.

Running with the ball using the inside of the foot

Traditionally the English game has relied more on 'inside of the foot' technique than the Continental style which has tended to prefer the outside of the foot, or 'front foot' techniques as they are now known.

Using the inside of the foot is a valid technique for running the ball, but it is not as athletic or fluent as the front foot method, nor does it integrate so smoothly with the execution of other skills. Nevertheless, in its favour is the security of operating with a larger surface and the benefit of having the ball close beneath the runner's body.

Inside foot control allows forward movement of the ball and at the same time a cross movement of the ball by playing it with each foot in turn. With practice it is an efficient way of running with the ball, keeping close control. When approaching an opposition player with the intention of beating him the advantage gained by continuous movement of the ball is to make it more difficult for the defender to time his tackle. When the ball is static or travelling in straight lines the task of winning the ball is made easier.

Moving the body across the ball

Moving the ball from one foot to the other is one way of making dispossession less likely. The other way is by moving the body across the ball or by swaying from one side of the ball to the other. The sway should follow the line of the ball but the trunk continues over to the outside of the foot that has controlled the ball.

Beating defender using inside foot dribbling techniques

Using the inside of the foot, players like the legendary Stanley Matthews would beat defenders by the straightforward use of rapidly changing pace. Matthews would move towards a full back slowly and then accelerate powerfully past him, dragging the ball inside with the right foot or outside with the left.

The feint with inside foot techniques

Moving the body across the ball while running with it is a good way of getting rhythm and of posing problems for defenders. It is also a way of preparing to use the feint.

To feint is to suggest with body movement you are going one way and then actually to go the other way. With the body already moving across the ball it is easy to accentuate one of the 'sways' at the right moment to upset the balance of the defender and then to bypass him when he has fallen for the trick.

Before making the feint it is best if the movements of the ball are short. This enables you to take advantage of your opponent's shift immediately.

Running with the ball using the outside of the foot

As mentioned earlier, outside of the foot techniques are referred to today as 'front foot' techniques, which is a description of the position of the ball when they are used.

The use of this technique has long been a neglected aspect of English football, whereas it characterizes the Continental way of moving. It has perhaps been the most important single factor in giving South American and Latin European football a greater elegance and fluency of movement, because quite naturally it contributes to a more athletic, more graceful co-ordination of the body. After all, it is more like the way we would run if there wasn't a ball at our feet.

The English preoccupation with the Chaplinesque position (or Penguinesque, as the former England manager, Ron Greenwood, has been known to refer to it) is thankfully diminishing as the younger breed of player, exposed to more enlightened coaching, is cultivating the ways of the Continentals.

Speed, agility and disguise cannot be accomplished adequately with the 'turned out' position, whereas the 'front foot' position lends itself to all these requirements. Furthermore, not to become proficient in the use of 'front foot' football is to restrict oneself to only 50 per cent of the potential moves and techniques open to the skilled dribbler.

Front foot running

Running with the ball using the outside of the foot requires a fine touch to ensure the ball does not stray too far from the controlling foot. It is, after all, already further from the player than it would be using the inside of the foot or 'back foot' technique.

To develop the technique of tight control with front foot running players should go on quick runs with the ball using the maximum number of touches they can over a measured distance. This develops the practice of 'feathering' the ball or just lightly touching it often to move it forward a short distance at a time.

A combination of front foot and back foot techniques

Front foot techniques combine well with 'inside foot' techniques, which can be used to bring the ball back on course should a player find he is veering away from the line he wants to take.

Beating a player

The combination of front and back foot techniques can also be used to beat a player.

By moving the ball forward and on a diagonal line with the front foot techniques the way is open, when challenged, to bring the ball back inside with the inside of the foot as the defender tackles.

Disguise

We have already said that front foot control can be done at greater speed because it integrates with natural running patterns, but it also has another strong advantage to recommend it: its facility for disguise.

To effect passes when playing with the inside of the foot certain changes in body position have to be made and these often divulge a player's intentions to a defender.

7 Over 20 metres the dribbler is using the outside of the playing foot to make contact as often as possible. To be successful the ball should travel no more than a third of a metre from the playing surface of the foot.

8 Using the outside surface of the right foot has taken the dribbler to the right. With one caress from the inside surface of the same foot he is back on course.

9 The dribbler on a right front foot run has brought the ball inside the tackler with the same foot.

10 A player running with front foot control can make a forward or diagonal pass with no alteration of posture other than a short back lift.

11 The dribbler with the ball on his right moving across to the right so that the ball is then on his left.

This is not so with front foot movement, where the quickest flick or pass can be given with the minimum of body alteration.

Moving the ball

As with back foot techniques, diagonal movement of the ball while running forward using the front foot serves to make a defender's job more difficult. Defenders are taught to 'watch the ball' and the more static it is the better they like it.

When dealing with back foot techniques we spoke of moving the body across the ball while running forward.

When running and using front foot techniques these two factors: **(a)** moving the ball from side to side and **(b)** moving the body across the ball are inseparable. As the song goes: 'You can't have one without the other'.

A heading duel in the FA Cup Final between Tottenham Hotspur and Queen's Park Rangers at Wembley in 1982. QPR's Hazell (no 5) gets the highest.

14

Movement of the ball using front foot techniques requires that the body comes across the ball to achieve it. Firstly we must deal with the movement of the ball.

To use the outside surfaces of both feet alternately in a dribbling run we have to think in terms of the opposition.

When the ball is on the right we use the outside surface of the left foot. To achieve this we have to move the body across the ball so that the ball is to the outside of the left foot. In other words, the ball itself just moves forward at this point but the body moves across it. Having moved to the right the ball is played to the left using the outside of the left foot. The player now moves across the ball in the opposite direction, still moving forward by virtue of a diagonal movement, so that the ball is to the outside of his left foot.

Imagine the problems running patterns of this sort pose for a defender – the ball is moving from side to side, the player is moving from side to side and because front foot techniques are being used the forward momentum is swift.

The target a young player should strive for is a full range of proficiency with all four foot surfaces used (the inside and outside of each foot). When he is efficient with all of them and has mastered fluent movement from one to the other at the appropriate time he is on the way to becoming a good dribbler and can practise the more precise skills contained in the following section.

12 The dribbler who has moved to the right with the ball outside the left foot playing the ball to the left.

13 The dribbler moving to the left so that the ball is to the outside of the right foot, being played diagonally to the right.

The Step-over

Eder *Brazil*

Eder is a very fast attacker who plays on the left side of the forward line, and has a screaming shot. He plays for Atlético Mineiro in Brazil. He scored a brilliant goal for Brazil against England at Wembley in 1981, and played in all Brazil's World Cup matches in Spain in 1982.

This skill can be executed standing still or on the run. The leading foot is brought explosively over the ball from the outside to the inside, giving the impression that a shot is being attempted. Having touched down just inside the ball, the outside of the foot sweeps the ball to the outside of the player, ready for a shot, a pass, or to continue the run. This skill is ideal for a raiding winger like Eder, as it creates the opening for a shot.

1 The player must be chest on to the ball with the ball in front of the controlling foot.

2 The controlling foot is moved swiftly over the ball from outside to inside. The whole body must intimate that a shot or pass is about to be made.

3 The controlling foot must touch the ground beyond the ball and to the inside of it.

4 Using the outside of the foot, the ball is swept outside of the normal line of the controlling leg.

5 Done properly the way should now be clear for advancement.

16

The Step-over and Outside Foot Flick

Eder *Brazil*

Eder is always alert to the play around him. Whether he has the ball or not he is poised for a quick run to the position where he will be most dangerous.

The Eder step-over is described in the previous skill. In this skill, when the foot has passed over the ball and landed to the inside of it the player swivels explosively on the heel, flicking the ball with the outside of the foot to a point diagonally or immediately behind him.

1 The controlling foot is passed explosively over the top of the ball from outside to inside.

2 The foot which is now on the ground is swivelled outwards and backwards on the heel, with the outside area of the foot making contact with the ball.

3 As the foot swivels on the heel so the body pivots round to the direction of the pass.

4 This skill is most useful when a player is being driven away from his objective, as a means of turning to beat a player or of setting up a wall pass situation.

The Step-over with Back Foot Drag

Eder *Brazil*

Eder in Brazilian strip during the 1982 World Cup Finals. He was part of a brilliant Brazilian forward line.

Sometimes the step-over will not work. An agile and alert opponent might not be fooled by the feint and might still be in a position to tackle as he was before the dummy. This particular skill is useful as a secondary manoeuvre to maintain progress should this happen. The step-over dummy is executed as in the previous skills. After the dummying foot has passed over the ball, the back foot drags through with the instep, making contact with the ball and knocking it on in front of the original dummying foot.

1 The player must be chest-on to the ball with the ball in front of the controlling foot.

2 The controlling foot is propelled swiftly over the ball from outside to inside. The whole body must intimate that a shot or pass is about to be made.

3 The controlling foot must touch the ground beyond the ball and to the inside of it.

4 At this point, with the dummying foot beyond and inside the ball, the back foot is dragged through to the ball, playing it with the outside and upper surface and pushing it forward.

5 Acceleration is important now and a good running pattern must be established quickly.

The Reverse Step-over

Mark Chamberlain *Stoke City*

Mark Chamberlain is an exciting young player who is a right-sided attacker for his club, Stoke City. With his speed and dribbling skills he operates like an old-fashioned right-winger, of which Stanley Matthews, who played for Stoke 50 years earlier, is an outstanding example. Chamberlain made his first appearance for England when coming on as a substitute against Luxembourg in the 1982-83 season.

In this skill, the components of the Eder step-over are reversed. The leading foot is brought explosively across the top of the ball from inside to outside and the ball swept inside using the instep. It is particularly effective when employed on the run, with an overlapping player used as a decoy, and a fast winger like Mark Chamberlain can leave his marker standing while he cuts in on goal with this skill.

1 The player must be chest-on to the ball with the ball in front of the controlling foot.

2 The controlling foot is pushed quickly over the ball from inside to outside the ball. The whole body must intimate that an outside of the foot pass is about to be made.

3 The controlling foot must touch down beyond the ball and to the outside of it.

4 Using the inside of the dummying foot, the ball is swept inwards in the direction of the standing foot.

Mark Chamberlain with the ball under close control for Stoke City.

The Reverse Step-over with Inside Foot Follow Through

Alan Brazil *Spurs*

Alan Brazil is a small attacking player who relies on speed and deft touches to score his many goals. He developed his career under Bobby Robson, later the England team manager, at Ipswich. He first played for Scotland as a substitute in 1980, and waited two years before his next cap. He played for Scotland in the World Cup finals in Spain, and later joined Tottenham Hotspur.

This skill differs from the previous skill, the Mark Chamberlain reverse step-over, in that the dummy is not expected to be 'bought'. Therefore the step-over is not explosive. After the foot has passed over the ball from inside to outside, the player continues in the same direction as the dummy, taking the ball with him, using the inside surface of the other foot. With the defender wrong-footed, a fast player like Alan Brazil manufactures the space he needs to continue his run or to shoot.

1 Execute the reverse step-over as described but do not make the dummy an explosive one.

2 The body weight will have been transferred to the dummying foot and this momentum should be continued.

3 The ball should now be pushed across the dummying foot with the other foot, using the inside surface of the instep.

4 Acceleration is now the key factor, having wrong-footed your opponent in this way.

The Reverse Step-over with Sole Pull

Glenn Hoddle *Spurs*

Glenn Hoddle is generally accepted by many English fans as being the most skilful player in the country, but for one reason or another in his international appearances he has rarely shown the complete authority he often displays in club games. He is a midfield player with great vision and manoeuvrability in tight situations, whose long-range distribution frequently sets colleagues free to run on goal. First capped in 1980, he played in some of England's World Cup matches in Spain in 1982 without establishing himself as an automatic choice.

The reverse step-over skill previously described is the first part of this skill. After the foot has passed over the ball from the inside to the outside, the sole pull is executed by the sole of the dummying foot pulling the ball back inside, across the standing foot. Glenn Hoddle uses this skill to keep his marker guessing while he chooses the best option for an attacking move.

1 Dummy to push the ball with the outside of the foot but pass the foot over the top of the ball. The foot should touch down just to the outside of the ball.

2 The trunk should be moved to suggest you intend to take the ball to your outside.

3 The sole of the dummying foot is now placed on top of the ball and rolled across the top, dragging the ball inside and across the standing foot.

Variation Where an opponent has not been fooled by the ploy, the ball can be switched back across the original playing foot with the instep of the original standing foot.

The Step-over and Reverse Step-over Combination

Paul Walsh *Liverpool*

Paul Walsh first attracted attention with some energetic goal-scoring displays for Luton Town in the 1982-83 season. He was taken on England's summer tour of Australia in 1983 and gained his first cap, pleasing manager Bobby Robson with a skilful performance. He is a direct player with a vast repertoire of swerves and feints. In 1984 he was transferred to Liverpool.

This is a compound skill where the step-over and the reverse step-over, previously described, are used. They can be linked in either sequence. Where the step-over is used first the sequence is foot over ball from outside to inside, moving the ball to a position outside the player. Then the same foot passes over the ball from inside to outside before sweeping the ball inwards, towards or past the standing foot. Executed at speed by a forward like Paul Walsh, it can bemuse the defender and clear a path to goal.

1 The player is chest-on to the ball, with the ball in front of the controlling foot.

2 The controlling foot is moved swiftly over the ball from outside to inside.

3 The controlling foot touches the ground beyond the ball and to the outside of it.

4 The movement is reversed, with the controlling foot passing over the ball from inside to outside.

5 Touching down the outside the ball, the controlling foot now sweeps the ball inwards towards or across the standing foot.

The Swivel

Trevor Francis *Sampdoria and England*

Trevor Francis was a prolific goal-scorer for Birmingham City from his first appearance at the age of sixteen. In 1979 he was transferred to Nottingham Forest, who became the first British club to pay another over £1 million for a player. He earned his first cap in 1977 when with Birmingham, continued playing for England while with Forest and Manchester City, and in July 1982 was bought by Sampdoria for £1,200,000 to play in Italy. He impressed in the World Cup finals in Spain in 1982 and continues to be England's most consistent and dangerous attacker.

This skill became a trade-mark of Johan Cruyff who used it to devastating effect in the World Cup finals of 1974, switching direction goalwards after being forced wide by a close-marking defender. It is a skill which Trevor Francis has incorporated into his repertoire with great success. Moving in one direction, he will feign to make a diagonal run in the opposite direction to the one in which he intends to go. He turns the ball back inside his standing foot, turning in the opposite direction to collect the ball and make for goal.

1 The player has his back to the target and is moving away from it.

2 Pivot on the standing foot, at the same time playing the ball with the inside toe area of the controlling foot.

3 The ball is played inside the standing foot and in the opposite direction to the dummy made earlier.

4 You then turn. If the ball is turned with the left foot, then you will turn to the right.

5 At the time of turning the ball and yourself you are balanced on the ball of the standing foot.

Steve Coppell and Trevor Francis celebrate an England goal.

The Pass Received and Swivel

Trevor Francis *Sampdoria and England*

Even when the ball is elsewhere, Trevor Francis follows the play ready to burst into action. He is one of the quickest footballers over the first few yards in the game today.

In this skill the player receives the pass with his back facing the target, i.e. the direction in which he wants to go. The pass is collected by the receiving foot and turned inside the standing foot, which has already begun to swivel. The swivel continues after the ball has been turned inside, so that the player ends facing his target with the ball in front of him. This skill is particularly useful for forwards facing their own goal and collecting a pass from defence. Trevor Francis uses it to steal a metre or two on a marker standing behind him.

1 The player faces the incoming pass which needs to be on the ground before the skill can be considered.

2 When the ball is within range of the playing foot swivel on the standing foot, making contact with the outside of the ball with the inside of the playing foot.

3 The ball is redirected inside the standing foot.

4 Continue to swivel on the standing foot to complete a half, or slightly more than a half, turn.

5 Collect the ball with the same foot as used originally to receive the ball at the outset.

The Ball Through Legs and Swivel

Trevor Francis *Sampdoria and England*

Trevor Francis of England in a difficult situation. The ball has come quickly to him at an awkward angle and he must get it under control before making his next move.

In this swivel skill the player turns his back on the ball to give the impression that he is allowing the ball to pass through his legs so that he can progress in the same direction as the pass. However he turns the ball back inside his standing leg while swivelling and proceeds in the opposite direction to that of the pass.

1 The player receives the pass and turns his back to the passer at the last minute. He must watch the ball throughout.

2 Give the impression that the ball will pass between the legs but allow it to go no further than the playing foot.

3 At this point turn the ball back inside the standing foot in the direction from which it came.

4 At the same time (3) is performed swivel on the standing foot, i.e. if the right foot is used to play the ball the left foot swivels, with the heel moving inwards.

The Step-over and Ride

Kenny Dalglish *Liverpool*

Kenny Dalglish was new Liverpool manager Bob Paisley's first important signing when he joined the Merseyside club from Celtic in 1977, with the task of replacing Kevin Keegan in Liverpool's attack. He has been an outstanding asset ever since and is known to Liverpool supporters as the 'King of the Kop'. Dalglish has won all the major honours with Liverpool. His strength lies in his vision and his skill in shielding the ball and performing sharp turns – which makes him particularly dangerous in the penalty area, where he scores many goals himself and makes them for others. He played for Scotland in the World Cup finals of 1974, 1978 and 1982.

This skill is a combination of a dummy and a pace absorber, or trap. It enables Dalglish to bring the ball under control in tight situations by persuading his marker to stand off, expecting a pass. The player approaches the oncoming ball sideways on, the leading leg is extended over the ball explosively to feign an outside of the foot pass, the ball is allowed to run to the inside of the back foot which absorbs the pace, riding round with the ball as the player pivots on the front foot.

1 Approach the ball sideways on.

2 The foot nearest the ball dummies to kick with the outside of the foot but passes over the top of the ball.

3 The ball follows through to the inside foot surface of the back foot.

4 The pivot on the front foot begins at the moment of contact between the back foot and the ball causing the back foot to guide the ball round in a U shape.

The Sway

Ossie Ardiles *Spurs and Argentina*

Ossie Ardiles was one of the stars of the Argentine side which won the World Cup in 1978. Shortly afterwards he was transferred from his club, Huracán, to Tottenham Hotspur in a deal which brought both him and his World Cup colleague, Ricardo Villa, to England for a joint fee of £750,000. He is a very busy creative midfield player who cleverly links defence to attack. His career at Spurs was interrupted by the war in the Falklands Islands, and he had a brief spell with the French club, Paris St Germain, before returning to White Hart Lane. He played for Argentina in the World Cup finals in Spain in 1982.

This skill is used when a player is being 'closed down' by an opponent. The player's legs are apart with the ball between the feet, as the player rocks from one foot to the other, touching each foot down close to the ball, until the opponent makes his move. The ball is then played to take advantage of the opponent's momentary shift. Ossie Ardiles, being small and with perfect balance, uses this skill to good effect.

1 The ball is on the ground. Position your feet apart with the ball between them.

2 Rock from side to side shifting off one foot and moving it away from the ball, moving the inside of the other foot to the side of the ball.

3 The trunk and head make a pronounced feint as though the ball is to be played across the standing foot.

4 If the opponent moved to cover the feint, then it is the inside of the standing foot which comes across and plays the ball in the opposite direction.

5 Several movements from side to side may have to be made before an opponent commits himself.

Karl-Heinz Rummenigge, twice European Footballer of the Year.

Sole of Foot Control

Paul Mariner *Arsenal*

Paul Mariner is a striker of great power and control, who combines mobility with skill on the ground and in the air. He joined Ipswich from Plymouth Argyle for £220,000 in 1976, being bought by Bobby Robson, the current England manager. He made his first appearance for England as a substitute in 1977, since when he has made over 30 appearances for his country and taken his goal tally into double figures. He played for England in all their matches in the 1982 World Cup Finals. In the 1983–84 season he left Ipswich Town for Arsenal.

This skill offers opportunities for all-round movement and allows change of control to take place very quickly. It is useful in crowded penalty areas and allows a striker like Paul Mariner to make those split-second decisions which frequently lead to a goal. The ball is pulled in different directions using the sole of the foot. The player must synchronize body movement with the movement of the ball, otherwise loss of balance will result.

1 The movement is best started with the ball at extended leg distance.

2 Pull the ball towards you and move to the side of the ball, keeping the same distance between yourself and the ball so as to be able to pull the ball into yourself again.

3 This routine continues as you pull the ball through to yourself at a variety of angles.

4 The pulling movements can be continuous or the ball can be stopped with the inside or outside of the foot.

5 The pull does not have to be straight back towards you. The ball can be pulled sideways, stroking the foot across the top of the ball from outside to inside.

Dribbling Using Both Outside Foot Surfaces

Mark Barham *Norwich City*

Mark Barham is a midfield attacking player who operates mainly on the right-hand side, although he likes to switch wings and raid with equal effect down either flank. He is a product of the very successful youth scheme at Norwich, and his skills were recognized when he was selected for England's summer tour of Australia in 1982-83, where he gained his first full cap.

An important feature of dribbling skills is rhythm. Good rhythm needs good balance and the poise to change direction swiftly and quickly. In this skill the outside surface of each foot is used alternately to provide the forward momentum necessary for a positive dribble. If the dribble is started with the right foot, the ball is pushed to the front and outside the player. The body is then brought across the ball so that the ball is to the outside of the left foot which then pushes it further forward, as the process is reversed.

1 Push the ball, using the outside foot surface, to the front of and outside the playing foot.

2 Bring the body across the ball so that the other foot has the ball to its outside.

3 Push the ball forward and outside the second playing foot.

4 Take the body across to the position it occupied in (1) and repeat this zig-zag movement until the pattern is established.

Backward Toe Roll

Bruno Conti *Italy*

Bruno Conti of Roma and Italy was an important member of the Italian side which won the World Cup in 1982. One of the most skilful players in the whole of the tournament, he impressed with runs down the flanks in the final against West Germany, but he is equally dangerous when he assumes a midfield role and makes his runs through the centre.

Often a player in possession is forced by opponents to go backwards. While retreating he usually tries to keep his body between the ball and the opponent. There are occasions, however, when the player in possession wants to tempt the opponent to 'bite' at the ball to create the space and opportunity to get behind him. Bruno Conti, being small and nippy, often uses this technique.

1 Place the toe area of the sole on the uppermost point of the ball.

2 Pull the foot backwards towards yourself, placing the playing foot back on the ground after each movement.

3 Because so much of this activity is on one foot the arms play an important role in stabilizing the body.

Variation After pulling the ball backwards several times it is advisable to introduce a linked forward movement to vary the tactic and to establish a pattern for reverse action.

Bruno Conti of Italy tackles Hans Peter Briegel of West Germany during the 1982 World Cup Final. Conti was one of the stars of the match.

The Aerial Dribble

Pelé *Brazil*

Pelé is the popular choice as the greatest player the world has ever seen. He is the only man to have played in three World Cup winning teams. In his career he scored over 1300 goals at an average of nearly a goal a game. There was not one aspect of the game of which Pelé was not the master. As well as being skilful and creative, he was strong and capable of surviving the toughest tackles. He could attack and defend, dribble and shoot and could control the ball with head or foot. He was always producing the unexpected, such as the shot from his own half which nearly scored in the 1970 World Cup tournament. A measure of his greatness is that over 90 songs have been written about him in various parts of the world.

This technique is a dribble where, instead of going round players with the ball on the ground, the ball is knocked over their heads and controlled on the other side of them. In the 1958 World Cup final, the 17-year-old Pelé scored a breathtaking goal after beating his man with just such a dribble. The move can be practised with real opponents or imaginary ones, in which case a marker or obstacle can be used to bring discipline to the exercise.

1 Knock the ball up from a pull and flick up (see Juggling Skill number 1).

2 Get several aerial touches in before using the technique for the mobile juggle described in Juggling Skill number 19.

3 At the first obstacle knock the ball just over the top. Where the player is imaginary, play the ball at a height above your own. Do not hit it too high as this will make control more difficult and you will have to wait longer for the ball to descend.

4 If you are concentrating on one foot when controlling the ball on the other side of the obstacle (opponent), then run to the opposite side of the controlling foot when you pass your opponent, e.g. with right foot control run to your left when rounding your opponent.

5 The technique for applying backspin to balls controlled in the air with the upper foot (Juggling Skill number 15) will help to absorb the pace of the dropping ball.

6 Pace can be absorbed by using the thigh on the other side of the obstacle.

The Cross Pull

Zico *Brazil*

Zico was the player the Brazilian fans looked to as the replacement for the brilliant Pelé. Perhaps this was asking too much of any player, and how far Zico fulfils these expectations is a matter of debate. He is, however, one of the greatest players in the world in his own right. In Brazil he plays for the championship-winning Flamengo side of Rio de Janeiro, Brazil's most popular team, whom British fans will remember for their 3-0 defeat of Liverpool in the World Cup Championship of 1981. Zico played with distinction for Brazil in the 1982 World Cup finals in Spain, scoring four goals. He was voted World Footballer of the Year in 1983.

The brilliant Zico uses this skill a lot for pulling the ball wide of a player coming in to tackle from the front. Running with the ball towards the tackler, the player leans his body to one side, away from the playing foot. Just before the tackle he pulls the ball wide towards the standing foot or beyond it, with the sole of his foot rolling sideways across the top of the ball.

1 Take the ball forward to an opponent, preferably using the outside of the foot.

2 Dummy to go even further to the outside just before reaching the opponent.

3 With the player off balance pull the ball inside towards the standing foot, using the sole.

4 By dragging the sole across the top of the ball and slightly down its outside surface the ball will roll across the playing foot and beyond the standing foot.

The Pull and Push

Diego Maradona *Argentina*

Maradona was capped for Argentina before his 17th birthday. He was still only 21 when in May 1983 Barcelona paid a world record transfer fee of £4,235,000 to secure his services. His stocky frame and bulky legs belie his athleticism and extraordinary mobility. An attacking forward, before the 1982 World Cup finals he was hailed as the best player in the world. Despite some great tussles with Italy's Gentile he had a disappointing tournament, which culminated in his being sent off. If his legs withstand the tough tackling he gets from most defenders, he should again establish himself as an all-time great.

Maradona is frequently tackled from the side and this trick is a favourite means of thwarting opponents. Imagine the player is running directly at goal and the opponent makes a run and attacks the ball from the side. Just before the moment of impact the player in possession drags the ball back towards himself, using the sole of the boot. The intention is to make the tackler miss the ball and overshoot his mark. The sole is rolled down the back of the ball, which is then push forward with the inside ball of the foot.

1 Forward dribble using the inside or outside of the foot.

2 As the player makes his attack from the side the sole is placed on top of the ball. The foot has been extended forwards to make this contact and will now drag the ball backwards to the rear of the standing foot. The action will stop when the foot has rolled right down the back of the ball to the ground.

3 Hopefully the opponent will have missed the ball and travelled across the front of the player in possession. At this point the ball is pushed forward with the inside ball of the foot.

4 The skill should be practised with a push-drag-push rhythm.

Diego Maradona, one of the world's most exciting players, shielding the ball from Brazil's midfield man, Falcao, during the World Cup match in 1982.

The Step-over and Play with Outside of Other Foot

Kevin O'Callaghan *Ipswich Town*

Although born in London, Kevin O'Callaghan plays for Eire, as his father is from Southern Ireland. He made 20 appearances for Millwall before moving to Ipswich for a fee of £250,000. A left-sided front player, who operates like an old-fashioned left-winger, he made his first international appearance in 1981. He is a fast and tricky player who likes to beat the full-back on the outside but can also cut in and shoot powerfully.

This skill is similar in its first stage to the reverse step-over skill of Mark Chamberlain described earlier. However, when the foot has passed over the ball from inside to outside, it is the outside of the other foot which comes across to take the ball in the opposite direction to the dummy.

1 The player is chest-on to the ball, with the ball in front of the dummying foot.

2 The dummying foot passes explosively over the top of the ball from inside to outside.

3 The dummying foot must pass further to the outside of the ball than it did for the Mark Chamberlain reverse step-over, and the body must lean and transfer weight to that foot.

4 The other foot is brought across so that the ball can be swept in the opposite direction to the dummy, using the outside surface of the foot.

The Glide Dummy

Karl-Heinz Rummenigge *West Germany*

For two years in succession, Karl-Heinz Rummenigge was top scorer in the Bundesliga, the German football league, and he was voted European Footballer of the Year in both 1981 and 1982. Like Kenny Dalglish of Liverpool, the Bayern Munich player is famed for turning half-chances into goals. He suffered an injury in the World Cup tournament of 1982, but few will forget the shot which hit the bar and nearly brought defeat for England. He was brought into the semi-final as a substitute, and scored, but could not turn out for West Germany in the final. He remains one of the most feared strikers in Europe.

This skill is used where the player approaches a pass across its line of play (i.e., the ball is passing in front of him). The nearest foot glides over the ball, which runs to the furthest foot, which plays the ball with inside surface in the direction of the glide. Strikers like Karl-Heinz Rummenigge use this technique to put a defender on the wrong foot and give themselves that fraction of a second which often leads to a goal strike.

1 Position the body diagonally to the incoming pass.

2 Move to the pass across its line of progress.

3 Play the nearest foot over the top of the ball in a casual manner.

4 The ball will pass through to the inside surface of the other foot, which plays the ball quickly in the direction of the original glide.

Basic Control Techniques

Basic control techniques are the starting point for any aspiring footballer. They are the prerequisite of order and fluency and without them frustration and chaos reign.

That control is an infinitely fascinating area of variety and colour this section of the book surely illustrates. Ways of controlling a football abound with range and invention, but for the formative footballer there are areas of very basic importance which must be mastered before the exciting journey into the upper strata of creativity can be explored.

Control starts at being able to to stop a ball that is propelled towards you on the ground. It progresses to being able to stop a ball that is delivered in the air. The next stage is to be able to take the pace off the ball and redirect it to advantageous positions, both on the ground and in the air. Arrival at this stage opens up a whole fertile area of skill and development. The ambitious player must be master of all the traps and pace-absorbers illustrated in this section.

Before venturing into this progression, however, and as an introduction to higher things, it should be of interest to the aspiring player to look at some of the basic control techniques and to understand how the components of them are essential to the development of more complex skills.

Falcao with the ball under control for Brazil in the World Cup match with Argentina.

Stopping the ball delivered along the ground

Square one of any control lesson looks a simple exercise; but is it? How often, even at top level, does it expose the deficiencies of experienced players? When the moving object hits an immovable surface control does not ensue. Only if the surface can be relaxed or withdrawn at the moment of impact, does any degree of control take place. Learning to use the controlling foot as a buffer or shock-absorber is the first stage in being able to control the ball.

As with passing, the safest way of controlling the ball with the foot is to offer the largest surface, and at first it will be the inside of the foot. Held squarely to the ball, it provides a large area of contact. When the ball arrives at the inside surface of the foot, control is dependent on three factors:

1 The accurate positioning of the foot in relation to the path of the ball.
2 The balance of the controlling player.
3 The optimum relaxation of the surface for the speed of the incoming ball.

The first factor is assisted by getting behind the line of the ball. This is a matter of infinite practice, so that the correct positioning becomes a reflex rather than a considered decision.

The second factor is partly innate but can be improved by coaching and awareness. Whenever a player is directly involved in the game he should be up on his toes and moving around in a state of readiness, much, once again, as a boxer would in the ring. It is the only way that good balance can be achieved. The football is a capricious object and any number of things can cause it to misbehave. A divot of turf can send it into a crazy dance, a gust of wind can change its path, or a degree of spin can accelerate or decelerate its progress unexpectedly. You can never tell, and it is always necessary to be on your guard.

The third factor comes entirely from practice. If the pace is to be taken from the ball, enabling the player to retain possession, it is necessary to absorb its pace by withdrawing the foot. In withdrawing the foot on contact, it is important to have extended it towards the ball in the first place and then to bring it back. It is not so easy to take it backwards from a normal standing position and still retain balance.

Exactly the same principles pertain when the ball played is in the air.

Once this stage has been reached the player is ready to start experimenting with pace absorption where the ball is redirected to another position. The most popular method of doing this, when the ball is approaching on the ground, is to extend the foot to the ball and, the moment contact is made, to swivel on the standing foot so that the ball rides round with the playing foot.

The same technique can be used for the ball that is delivered off the ground, providing it is not higher than waist level.

When the ball is at waist height then the thigh surface can be used in the same manner, but not with exactly the same movement pattern. When the thigh is extended to the ball on impact it is pulled backwards and out very

14 The foot extended.

15 The foot relaxed on impact.

16 The ball approaching at knee level.
The player meets it with his foot extended.

17 The player swivelling on the standing foot so that the ball played to him at knee level

rides round with the playing foot.

18 The thigh control with swivel.

quickly and the ball will drop behind the player, who swivels immediately the skill has been performed.

Where the ball comes in at chest height, then the chest can be used to divert the ball to the side but it is very difficult to get a full turn with the ball by relaxing the surface of the chest and swivelling.

There are players in England who use the head in the extended-relaxed sequence to take pace off the ball. One player who uses this technique expertly is Paul Mariner.

19 Trapping the ball between the inside arch of the foot and the ground.

Traps

The orthodox and most used trap in English football is the technique whereby the ball is trapped between the inside arch of the foot and the ground. The reason for the efficiency of this trap is once again that it affords a large safe surface with which to control the ball.

The same principle applies when the outside of the foot surface is used but this needs a great deal more practice and experience, since timing and accurate placing of the foot are far more crucial with this method.

Another very safe, though not very elegant, trap is the use of the sole.

The ball is trapped between the sole of the boot and the ground. The tendency for inexperienced users of this method is to bring the whole of the sole down on to the ball which makes it a very cumbersome technique indeed. All that is really needed is for the foot to be lifted partially at the front, without very much movement of the leg at all. If the ball is dropping vertically then the sole trap should not be used. Such a ball should be controlled with the top foot pace absorber or the thigh pace absorber.

The thigh pace absorber is another fairly elementary technique which ought to be mastered at an early stage. As mentioned it is an ideal skill for dealing with the vertically falling ball. It merely requires that the surface is offered to the ball and relaxed on impact. On this occasion 'relaxed' means 'withdrawn', so that the pace is taken out of the ball and it drops to the ground.

Once the young player is skilled at these elementary traps and pace absorbers, he can develop the second-stage control techniques contained in the following sections.

20 The outside of the foot trap.

21 The sole trap. **22** Using the thigh to absorb pace.

Paul Mariner causes a diversion in the Spanish wall at a free-kick in England's World Cup match with Spain in 1982.

The Top Foot Pace Absorber

Socrates *Brazil*

Socrates is an intelligent and skilful player whose club is Corinthians of São Paulo. He was captain of Brazil in the 1982 World Cup finals in Spain. Had Brazil won he would almost certainly have retired from football to pursue his profession as a doctor, but since Brazil, the choice of most fans as the most attractive footballing side in the tournament, were eliminated in the second stage Socrates might remain in the game for one more try. He has over 30 caps and enjoys taking penalties, it being said that he has taken over 50 without missing one. Socrates plays in the centre of midfield, where he is a very commanding captain, lending his talent to both defence and attack.

The first principle of this skill is to get the body into the flight of the ball. It can be used when the ball has a gentle trajectory or when it has been hit with pace, since the object is not to catch the ball but to arrest its impetus. For a player heavily involved in midfield like Socrates this is a necessary skill, as he is required to control balls coming from all angles at all speeds.

1 Get the body in line with the descent of the ball, and align leg and foot to the flight path.

2 Extend the control surface towards the ball.

3 On impact withdraw the playing surface, using it as a brake.

4 Just before the controlling foot reaches the ground the toes are pointed downwards to deliver the ball to the ground.

The Top Foot Catch

Ramon Diaz *Argentina*

Ramon Diaz is an attacking player who plays for River Plate in Argentina. He came into the national side after the World Cup victory in 1978, making his debut against Yugoslavia in 1979. In the 1982 World Cup finals in Spain he played in all but one of Argentina's matches, but did not play a full game, either being taken off for a substitute or being a substitute himself.

In this skill the ball is caught between the upper surface of the toes and the shin. The foot is raised to the ball and relaxed on impact to absorb the pace, making it possible to clamp the ball before the controlling foot touches the ground. It enables the attacker, like Diaz, to achieve perfect control over the ball, even though he might be surrounded by defenders.

1 When starting to practise this skill, the ball should not drop from a great height.

2 It is important that the catching surface and the ball are in line.

3 The foot should be lifted to the dropping ball.

4 At the point of impact it should be relaxed with the ball to absorb the pace.

5 Before the foot is lowered the upper foot should be snapped back towards the shin clamping the ball.

The Top Foot Pace Absorber (Scissor Movement) With the Ball Taken Through Legs

Alain Giresse *France*

Alain Giresse is captain of the French team, Bordeaux. Although now in his thirties he is a pocket dynamo of a player. France was one of the surprise teams of the World Cup finals in Spain in 1982, where they lost the semi-final, rather unluckily, on penalties. Alain Giresse, in midfield, excelled and was one of the best players in an excellent team.

This skill is performed when the ball has a gradual descent. The ball is taken from the air with a scissor movement and guided down between the legs ready for the player to turn and begin a movement in the chosen direction. It is a spectacular movement of value to fast, busy midfielders like Alain Giresse, who can take an aerial pass from defence and turn to begin an attack with the ball under control.

1 The body has to be in the line of flight of the ball.

2 The controlling surface is extended towards the ball after the standing leg has kicked upwards in a scissor movement.

3 The playing surface is relaxed upon impact, acting as a brake and guiding the ball down inside the standing leg which has not yet reached the ground.

4 The ball is allowed to drop off the playing foot when it has reached a point behind the standing foot which has been thrown forward.

5 Finally turn and move off with the ball.

The Catch Trap Transferred to Other Foot

Arnold Muhren *Manchester United and Holland*

Arnold Muhren was signed from the Dutch club, Twente Enschende, by Bobby Robson, now England manager, when he was manager of Ipswich Town in 1978. He joined Manchester United and at the beginning of the 1983-84 season showed a happy knack of scoring vital goals, a bonus to add to his midfield skills of accurate passing and the ability to deny possession to opposing players.

In this skill the top foot catch, as described earlier, is executed. Stability and good balance are necessary before the transfer from one foot to another can be achieved. Once the ball has been trapped by the first foot, it is thrown upwards from the foot to a distance of about half a metre (18 inches). The second foot is taken up to the ball and on contact relaxed with the ball's descent and the ball clamped against the shin. In practising, once a rhythm has been established, the ball can be transferred from foot to foot. This skill can be performed with a forward movement, with the player approaching goal in this manner, although it might infuriate a manager or coach as it is of limited use in a match situation. Performed sparingly, by a player with the control skills of Arnold Muhren, the movement provides surprise for the marker and gives the player a split second of time to choose his next move.

1 The catching foot is lifted to the dropping ball.

2 Once the ball has been trapped by the catching foot it is thrown upwards and over in the direction of the second foot.

3 The second foot is now taken up to the ball and on contact holds the ball against the shin.

4 You are now ready to transfer the ball back to the first foot or to make progress with the ball under control.

The Cross-legged Outside Foot Trap

Ray Wilkins *AC Milan and England*

A Londoner, Ray Wilkins began his career with Chelsea, and showed such form and awareness that he was club captain of the first division side when only 18 years old. An attacking midfield player, he made his debut for England in 1976. He was transferred to Manchester United in 1979 for £825,000, scoring a spectacular goal in the FA Cup final in 1983. He captained England until suffering an injury, and played in all England's matches in the 1982 World Cup finals in Spain. In 1984 he was transferred to AC Milan and went to play in Italy.

In this trap the controlling foot passes across the front of the standing foot. The ball is trapped with the outside of the foot and swept across the standing foot. The ball can be dropped to the ground at its original point of impact. This skill is particularly good for screening and keeping a distance between an opponent and the ball. Ray Wilkins is adept at screening the ball and this skill enables him to control a difficult ball and leave himself room to manoeuvre.

1 The chest is square-on to the flight path of the ball. The trapping leg is swept across the standing leg just below the knee.

2 The outside area of the instep is used to control the ball.

3 The higher the surface of the ball addressed the more complete the trap. This is the best method when the ball is being left at its original point of impact. Where the ball is being swept across the standing foot, it should be played just below the horizontal mid-line of the ball.

The Concave Chest Trap

Tony Woodcock *Arsenal*

Tony Woodcock played for Nottingham Forest under Brian Clough, gaining a European Cup winners' medal in 1979, before being transferred to FC Cologne in 1980. He made his England debut while with Forest and won several more caps with Cologne before returning to England to play for Arsenal. A dangerous striker, he is noted for his quick control and accurate shooting in the penalty box.

This technique is best used when the incoming ball is rising or approaching the player at a level height. It is an invaluable skill, particularly when the ball comes directly to an attacker from a rebound or half-clearance, as it enables quick control which positions the ball for a snap shot, and this is why it is a speciality of Tony Woodcock. The shoulders are brought forward and the back is rounded to absorb the speed of the ball on the chest. The trunk is tilted forward and the ball directed downwards.

1 Get in the flight path of the ball and be ready to adjust your height. The chest needs to be over the ball. This may mean having to jump or bend at the knees.

2 The chest is extended towards the ball. On impact the shoulders are snapped forward to produce an absorbent surface for the ball to hit.

3 At the same time as you snap the shoulders forward the trunk is tilted forward directing the ball downwards.

4 The greater the degree of tilt by the trunk the closer to the feet the ball will land.

The Instep Trap at the Back of the Standing Foot

Kevin Keegan *Newcastle United*

Kevin Keegan began his career at Scunthorpe and was brought to Liverpool by Bill Shankly. He was an immediate success and became a favourite of the 'Kop'. He spent six years at Liverpool, winning many honours, principally a European Cup winners' medal in 1977. He was England's Footballer of the Year in 1976. After the European Cup win he was transferred to Hamburg and in 1978 and 1979 was voted European Footballer of the Year. He was an automatic choice for England and was captain for some years. Injury before the 1982 World Cup finals in Spain prevented him playing a part – he came on as substitute in the final drawn game with Spain, his 63rd cap. He returned to England to play for Southampton and was then transferred to Newcastle United.

In this skill the dropping ball is controlled by the inside surface of the instep, the controlling leg crossing behind the standing leg. The trapping foot is turned with the toes pointing towards the standing foot with the heel uppermost. It is a difficult skill which enables closely-marked players, as Keegan always was, to play the ball and attack the goal before the marker can get in a tackle.

1 At the time of contact with the ball the chest is diagonal to the flight path of the ball.

2 The trapping leg is bent at the knee and crossed behind the standing foot with the toe on the ground and the heel held approximately 15 cm (six inches) off the ground. The standing foot is turned diagonally away from the area of control.

3 The arch of the foot with the heel held off the ground presents a trapping area for the ball to be controlled.

4 The degree to which the ball is 'killed' or allowed to partially escape is determined by the angle of the heel, *e.g.* where the heel is upright in relation to the toes the ball will escape the back spin, where the heel is forward and inclined the ball will be trapped decisively.

5 Escape is a useful component where the ball requires redirection, e.g. to bring the ball round the standing foot to the original position of the trapping foot.

Kevin Keegan – all-action player with many clubs in England and on the Continent.

Convex Chest Trap with Ball Rolling Down Body

Michel Platini *France*

Michel Platini has for many years been the most popular player among French soccer followers. Born in 1955, he played for Nancy and St Etienne before joining the Italian club Juventus. He has been a regular fixture in the national side and played a significant part in France's outstanding performances in the 1982 World Cup, when they were unlucky not to reach the final. A forward with close control, Platini specializes in scoring from free-kicks. He was European Footballer of the Year in 1983.

With this skill the ball is trapped by the chest in a way that prevents it bouncing away towards an opponent. It enables high balls to be controlled in the minimum of space and is essential for players like Platini who have to operate in crowded areas and frequently with close markers. The player sticks out his chest to receive the ball, and on impact snaps the shoulders and arms forwards. The back is arched to present a platform for the ball to roll off down the body to the thigh.

1 Get in the line of flight of the ball.

2 Extend the chest towards the ball, at the same time as arching the back to provide a platform for the ball to fall on to. The chest should be stuck out with the shoulders back.

3 On impact the shoulders are snapped back, still retaining the arched back.

4 Where a player has jumped or gone on to tip-toe this will all help to absorb the pace as the player returns to the ground.

5 Straightening of the back will cause the ball to roll off the chest and down to the thigh, the upper foot or the ground.

The Thigh Bounce

Marco Tardelli *Italy*

Marco Tardelli has not looked back since leaving the Italian second division club Como in 1975 to join Juventus. Over 50 caps for Italy followed, and he played a big part in the World Cup success of 1982. A midfield player, he is frequently at odds with referees, as he combines a ruthless streak with his undoubted skills.

The thigh bounce is a delivery skill, the thigh being used to project the ball to other surfaces where it can be played again. Midfield players like Tardelli need the skill in order to control the ball quickly and begin attacking movements. The fleshy part of the thigh is used to control and divert the dropping ball to the feet or chest, or to a team-mate close by.

1 The player should be in a direct line with the ball for good balance. Under pressure he may line the controlling surface (the thigh) with the ball without movement of the whole body.

2 The controlling surface should be moved to the ball at a speed commensurate with the degree of bounce required, *i.e.* the faster the thigh action and the more follow through, then the further and quicker the ball will travel.

3 The ball can be bounced to the chest by using follow through. The extent to which this is used will be determined by the speed and trajectory of the incoming ball.

4 To divert a ball to the side of a player, the thigh will be rotated at the hip to the appropriate side.

5 This skill should not be confused with the Thigh Trap where withdrawal of the playing surface takes the pace off the ball.

Simon Stainrod, a goal-scoring forward for his club, Queen's Park Rangers.

The Gluteus Maximus Trap

Simon Stainrod *Queen's Park Rangers*

Simon Stainrod joined Queen's Park Rangers after spells with Sheffield United and Oldham Athletic. An entertaining and skilful player, he is always ready to try the unorthodox, and, when successful, he pleases the Loftus Road crowd in the Rodney Marsh and Stan Bowles tradition. Despite his penchant for the unusual, he is serious about his talent for scoring goals and his 24 led the club's goal-scoring list in the 1981-82 season. He was an important member of the team which won promotion to the first division in 1982-83.

This skill can be employed when the ball approaches from the rear, whether directly or diagonally. The ball must have a steep descent for the skill to be practicable. The ball is trapped after it has bounced and begun to rise, by the player's posterior being placed above the ball to prevent its escape. The skill raises a laugh which appeals to crowd-pleasers like Simon Stainrod, but it is a perfectly legitimate way of controlling a bouncing ball, particularly on the high-bouncing artificial turf at Loftus Road.

1 The ball is controlled with this skill when it approaches the player from the rear.

2 The steeper the descent the closer you have to be to the point where the ball bounces. Where the descent is shallow you do not have to be so close. Experimentation will clarify the positions that need to be taken up in relation to the trajectory of the incoming ball.

3 The knee joint is flexed, lowering the fleshy area at the top of the thigh towards and over the rising ball.

4 The fleshiness of the controlling surface will be sufficient to absorb the momentum of the ball and return it to the ground ready for the ensuing skill.

Back Spin Chip and Dummy Through Legs

Jean Tigana *France*

Jean Tigana's career blossomed when he was transferred from Toulon to Lyon in 1978. After a big-money move to Bordeaux he began to attract the attention of the French selectors. In the World Cup finals of 1982 he appeared as a substitute in France's first game against England, played in all the second-phase matches, and was one of the stars of the epic semi-final against West Germany.

This skill has two essentials: the ball must be approaching along the ground and it must be at medium or medium-fast pace. When the ball approaches the player it is struck centrally to produce spin which returns the ball back towards the player, who allows the ball to pass between his legs, turning to collect it and proceed. It is a skill which is executed at speed and is a useful weapon for such fast, busy players as Tigana.

1 The ball is received on the ground at medium or fast pace. Anything slower will not produce sufficient spin for the skill to succeed.

2 When the ball approaches the playing foot the player stabs centrally beneath the ball with the toes producing the spin, which causes the ball to rotate back towards the player.

3 The player allows the ball to pass between his legs before swivelling on whichever foot he chooses and collecting the ball with his back to its original point of service.

4 Where the player has used his right foot and turns to the left, the controlling surface on completion of a half turn will be the inside of the right foot: where the player turns to the right, the controlling surface will be the outside of the right foot.

The Inside Foot Ride

Alan Sunderland *Ipswich*

Alan Sunderland has been a consistent and talented performer for both Wolves and Arsenal without getting the nod from the England selectors. He had made 158 appearances for Wolves and scored 29 goals when Arsenal signed him for £200,000 in 1977. His goal scoring increased with his new club, where a similar number of appearances produced 45 goals, including the last-minute winner which won the FA Cup for Arsenal 3-2 against Manchester United in 1979.

This skill is used for controlling direct passes at a player whether on the ground or up to 60 cm (2 ft) off it. The inside of the foot is used to take the pace off the ball and act as a brake, taking the ball past the standing foot at a controlled pace, the standing foot pivoting so that the player faces the dead ball. It is a useful skill for front players like Alan Sunderland, who receive the ball in a variety of trajectories, usually with a marker in close attendance.

1 The controlling foot is turned out so that the inside surface of the instep is presented squarely to the ball.

2 The surface is extended to the oncoming ball and on impact, is withdrawn, riding the ball close to the controlling foot and past the standing foot.

3 The player now pivots on the standing foot so as to complete a half turn.

4 The ball by now should have stopped or slowed and the player is ready to apply the next skill.

Bryan Robson, attacking midfield player for Manchester United and England.

Back Spin with the Ball Circling Outside Player

Liam Brady *Sampdoria and Eire*

Liam Brady is a creative midfield player with a very elegant style who played for many years with Arsenal. There he established himself as an inventive and highly entertaining player, who was the midfield general of the side. In 1979 he moved to Juventus in Italy for a fee of £500,000, and in 1983 went on to Sampdoria. He made his first appearance for Eire in 1975 and has remained perhaps their most talented player and an automatic choice since.

This skill is best performed when the ball is on the ground and travelling at medium pace. The player moves to the ball, dummies to kick it diagonally in the direction whence it came, but strikes through the extreme inside of the ball, slicing it to apply spin. The ball spins back around the player for him to turn and collect. It is a precise skill which players of the command of Liam Brady can use to get away from a defender on either side of them.

1 Move to the ball sideways on, chest facing the direction which is opposite to the intended route of the ball.

2 Slice through the extreme inside of the ball, causing the ball to spin outwards, rotating in the direction the ball will take.

3 The player has two options when it comes to turning. Firstly he can turn away from the spin and possibly round his opponent, or he can take the same route as the ball, hoping that the initial dummy has caused the opponent to move to the opposite side.

4 The foot surface to be used is the extreme outside of the little toe and the outside ball of the foot.

Ball Through Legs and Inside Foot Turn

Steve Archibald *Spurs and Scotland*

Steve Archibald began his career in Scottish football with Clyde, moving to Aberdeen in 1977. Tottenham paid £800,000 for him in 1980, buying Garth Crooks from Stoke City at the same time to form a brand-new striking partnership. The combination was immediately successful, the club winning the FA Cup in 1981 and 1982. In his first season at Spurs Archibald scored 25 goals. He made one appearance for Scotland as a sub in 1980 while still with Aberdeen, and rapidly established himself in the side, playing in the 1982 World Cup finals.

This skill is used when the ball is played on the ground at moderate speed. The player turns his back to the ball and dummies to kick with the outside of the foot, but passes the foot over the ball, allowing it to roll between his legs. As the ball passes the standing foot it is turned inwards by the controlling foot, using the inside of the foot. The skill enables a striker like Steve Archibald to change the direction of the ball and proceed without stopping it.

1 Just before receiving the pass turn your back to the ball.

2 Pass the playing foot over the ball, pretending to kick it with the outside of the foot.

3 The ball will roll between the dummying foot and the standing foot. At this point it is turned inwards across the front of the standing foot, using the inside of the instep.

The Overhead Chip-kick

Ricardo Villa *Fort Lauderdale and Argentina*

Ricardo Villa was a member of Argentina's 1978 World Cup-winning team, shortly afterwards signing for Spurs in a joint transfer deal with Ossie Ardiles. He became a favourite with Spurs fans without quite establishing an automatic place in the side. A big but elegant player, his dribbling seemed sometimes deliberate, but it was very effective and his breathtaking dribble past four opponents to score the winning goal for Spurs in the 1981 FA Cup Final was one of the best goals seen at Wembley. He now plays for Fort Lauderdale in the North American Soccer League.

This technique is best performed when the ball is static, especially at set pieces, where the defence has formed a well-constructed wall. The player taking the kick approaches the ball as if to play it beyond the wall. He has his own player behind him and chips the ball straight back over his own head for his colleague to volley or half-volley at goal. This skill is suitable for masters of the dead ball like Ricky Villa.

1 Approach the ball in a way that totally conceals your intentions.

2 Point the toe downwards and get the foot as far under the ball as possible.

3 The ball is lifted with an action similar to that of pedalling a bicycle backwards. The leg is fairly straight as the action begins, but bends increasingly at the knee as the ball is lifted higher.

4 To facilitate clearance over the player's head the player needs to lean backwards as much as possible.

Bryan Robson and Phil Thompson of England attempting to stop Karl-Heinz Rummenigge of West Germany in the goalless draw in the 1982 World Cup Finals.

Convex Chest Trap to a Top Foot Catch

Bryan Robson *Manchester United and England*

Bryan Robson became Britain's most expensive player when Manchester United manager, Ron Atkinson, bought him from his old club, West Bromwich Albion, for £1.5 million in 1981. A lorry driver's son, Robson became a strong midfield player with a command of all aspects of the game, including that of scoring vital goals. He scored the fastest goal of the World Cup finals when he netted for England against France in 27 seconds. He made his first appearance for England in 1980, and after captaining West Bromwich Albion and Manchester United he has now established himself as captain of the national side.

This is a combination trapping sequence, used with a dropping ball. The chest is thrown forward to receive the ball and upon impact is extended, with a short explosive movement, to enable the ball to be popped upwards and forwards. The dropping ball is met with the controlling foot which on impact is withdrawn to absorb the pace of the ball. At a point about half a metre (18 inches) from the ground the ball is caught between the toes and the shin. With this skill Bryan Robson can have a difficult ball under perfect control without a tackler being able to make a challenge.

1 Get behind and under the flight path of the dropping ball.

2 Bend backwards to present the chest as a platform on which the ball can drop.

3 The extension of the chest is achieved by snapping the shoulders back vigorously, thereby throwing the chest forward and popping the ball into the air.

For the components of the Top Foot Catch see the Ramon Diaz skill described earlier in this section.

The Convex Chest Trap, Thigh Bounce and Top Foot Catch

Willy Miller *Aberdeen and Scotland*

Willy Miller is a centre back who combines with McLeish to form a solid rearguard for Aberdeen and blends with equal effectiveness with Alan Hansen in the centre of the Scottish defence. He has been a vital part of Aberdeen's recent successful run which culminated in victory in the European Cup-winners Cup in 1983. He made his first appearance for his country against Rumania in 1975 and played in the World Cup finals in Spain in 1982.

This is another combination skill which introduces a thigh bounce into the previous skill. The ball is popped off the convex chest to the thigh. The thigh meets the dropping ball to bounce it upwards again to drop to the controlling foot, which is raised towards the ball and which relaxes on impact to absorb the pace and catch the ball between top foot and shin. It is useful to a central defender like Willy Miller when he is receiving a ball pumped downfield by the opposition and has plenty of time to control it. It enables maximum control without the risk of the ball bouncing away towards an onrushing forward.

All the skills needed for this sequence have already been individually described. A difficult feature of this combination sequence is linking the skills together. Maximum pace needs to be taken from the ball on each contact so that the ball is travelling slowly at all times. The use of the arms in maintaining balance is of extreme importance since most of the skill is conducted on one leg.

Shooting and Passing

Passing is the essential mobility of football. Without it the game becomes a dislocated series of melees which occur in different areas of the field because people have run the ball there.

The shape, the fluency and the continuity of the game depend on good passing. It is easy to see the shape of football without good passing when we watch young sides who do not have the strength or the proficiency to move the ball from one player to another by means of good passing techniques.

Passing is, ostensibly, the easiest of the game's techniques to master, yet strangely it is the most consistently malpractised aspect of the game.

Top-class teams of highly paid professionals can play a whole game without stringing together a sequence of passes worthy of the name possession. School teams rarely manage an uninterrupted passing sequence of above four passes and in the very young player the link-up almost never gets above two passes.

Why then are there so many problems in attaining proficiency in this seemingly simple aspect of the game?

To start with, good passing relies to a great extent on good supporting positions. Unless players without the ball have a clear understanding of how to position themselves in relation to the player with the ball, the possibility of sustained passing movements becomes remote.

The two factors that affect good support are angle and distance. If the angle of the player in support is not right then accessibility is lost.

Similarly, if the distance between the player with the ball and the player in support is incorrect then the likelihood of failure increases dramatically. A player can select a good angle to support the ball but if his position is too close to the player with the ball, then he is as vulnerable to the marking player as his colleague who already has possession. Equally, it is as negative to take up a support position which is unnecessarily distant and does not achieve penetration.

Norman Whiteside of Northern Ireland gets in a shot at the French goal, despite the efforts of defenders to intercept in the World Cup second-phase matches of 1982.

23 (a) A poor support position. (b) a good support position.

A third factor which has to be considered, and which contradicts the point about angles, is an awareness of the range and proficiency of the player with the ball. For example, what may appear to be a disastrous angle could, with a player who is excellent at chipping, turn out to be a wonderful support position.

Although good support positions are important, they will be no use, however perfect, if the passing techniques are not proficient. Breakdowns will occur with frustrating regularity.

Therefore it is most important, when developing passing skills, to introduce a wide range of techniques. So many situations break down, even at the top level, because players do not possess sufficient breadth of technique to be able to extricate themselves from the various pressures placed upon them in matches.

As with dribbling and control we start by looking at the techniques most widely used. They are the safe techniques because they minimize the risk factor.

In passing, the inside of the foot technique is generally preferred because it affords a large surface with which to make contact with the ball. The inside of the foot pass can be compared with the use of a croquet stick; it is a fairly infallible lever which can swing through the ball and move it from one place to another, without the risk of ricochets inherent in other techniques.

However, like everything else there are 'fors' and 'againsts'.

The main drawback of the pass with the inside foot is the lack of disguise. The playing surface has to be 'turned out' so that it can be used, and this imparts tell-tale signs to opposition players and makes it less attractive than the outside or front foot pass.

That is not to say the technique is completely devoid of the principle of disguise. There are ways of angling the body to suggest alternatives, just as there are ways of applying the technique late, and these help to camouflage a player's intentions.

Inside of the foot passing is especially advisable when the ball is travelling towards the passer and a first-time pass is to be made.

First time passing with the inside surface

There are four main requisites for good passing.

1 Agility and balance. A player must be on his toes so that he can make the minute adjustment needed to get into a good position.

So often when players are using the inside surface the back foot is anchored and the playing foot is left to make all the adjustments to a changed trajectory or an acceleration or fall-off of pace.

A dancing agility very much like that which a boxer uses in negotiating the ring is ideal for ensuring balance and mobility.

2 The player must get behind the line of the incoming ball.

3 At the moment of contact the player should get close to the ball. Stretching to make contact loses balance and causes the player to lean back, which will in turn cause the ball to lift.

4 The ball should be struck through the middle, with the knee over the ball and the standing leg slightly flexed.

24 Passing the ball. Notice the passer is close to the ball, and is playing through the ball with the standing leg slightly flexed and the arms giving balance.

25 (a) The contact area of the ball for the conventional pushed pass.
(b) The contact area of the ball for achieving swerve.

Swerve and the inside foot pass

Both the inside foot and the outside surfaces are conducive to applying swerve to passes.

Swerve is an essential element of a comprehensive range of passing techniques. Defenders take up strategic positions to stop attackers getting the ball into crucial space. Good defenders are aware of where the vulnerable zones are and they are also aware of the running patterns, even when these take place behind them.

Apart from chipping and lifting the ball, swerve is the only technique that a player can use to gain access to these important areas of the pitch.

The inside foot pass with swerve is achieved by making three pronounced changes from the 'pushed' pass in the way the ball is addressed.

Firstly, the contact area of the ball differs in that, instead of playing through the ball centrally, the outside edge of the ball becomes the contact area.

Secondly, the part of the foot used to address the ball changes.

Thirdly, the line of approach and follow through also alters.

The same principles of approach and follow-through apply to volleyed and half-volley passes.

26 (a) The approach for the pushed pass is straight towards the ball and straight through it.
(b) The approach for the swerved pass is diagonally across the ball from inside to outside.

Outside of the foot passing techniques

The advantage of inside foot passing techniques, namely the larger contact area, is offset to a large degree by its extra predictability and its awkwardness in the athletic sense. It does not integrate smoothly with running patterns. The player running with the ball has to alter his stance very little to pass the ball when it is on the front foot and the pass is being made with the front foot. There is not the studied turning out of the playing surface which has to occur with back foot passing.

Where swerve needs to be used the front foot technique is, once again, preferable because it integrates smoothly with the running action.

These are the basic passing techniques but outside of these staple methods there exists a wide range of more complex but, nevertheless, extremely effective skills which come under the heading of passing. These are developed in detail in the following section, together with the techniques of shooting.

27 (a) The front foot pass.   (b) The back foot pass.   **28** The front foot swerved pass.

Paolo Rossi of Italy, the leading scorer in the 1982 World Cup Finals, who scored a hat-trick against Brazil.

The Bent Ground Shot (Inside Foot)

Charlie Nicholas *Arsenal and Scotland*

The goal-scoring feats of Charlie Nicholas for Celtic in the Scottish Premier League in the 1982-83 season marked him as a player of exceptional talent who interested clubs all over the world. Arsenal secured his signature, and his appearances for Scotland in the Home International Championship of 1983 and his first appearances for Arsenal in the 1983-84 season were watched with great interest. An attacker of great potential, he could develop into a world-class player in the 1980s.

Passes or shots are bent for three reasons: to get the ball around obstacles such as a well-positioned opponent, to turn the ball into the path of a running team-mate, and to make it difficult for opponents to anticipate the trajectory of a pass or shot. In this skill, the ball is spun in an anti-clockwise direction (looking from the top at a right-foot shot) by kicking the ball on the outside with inside instep. Charlie Nicholas uses the skill both for passing and shooting.

1 From dead ball situations and for extreme spin the approach should start from a position well inside the position of the ball. This enables the back outside area of the ball to be hit. On the run, when extreme spin is required, the foot has to be moved diagonally across in relation to body position, to compensate for being directly behind the ball.

2 For ground shots or passes the ball needs to be kicked through the horizontal mid-line and to the extreme outside of the vertical line. The foot surface for this kick is the inside instep at the base of the big toe.

3 The line of follow-through depends on the degree of spin we are trying for. Limited spin requires the foot to follow through the side of the ball while extreme spin requires a diagonal follow through more to the back of the ball. You should familiarize yourself with the relationship between power, spin and distance, e.g. when you hit a ball with x amount of power and address the ball at a particular point, what is the curve of the ball and is it sufficient to round a wall standing at 10 metres and enter a goal at 35 metres?

The Bent Ground Shot (Outside Foot)

Paolo Rossi *Italy*

Paolo Rossi was brilliant in Italy's 1982 World Cup victory in Spain. The Juventus star returned to the side after two years suspension imposed after an illegal betting scandal and played as if he had never been away. Rossi had also endured four cartilage operations. He made his debut for Italy in December 1977, and in the 1978 World Cup in Argentina was voted second best player behind Kempes. He scored three goals on that occasion, and his six goals in three games, including a hat-trick against Brazil in 1982, mark him as a remarkable striker.

This skill is practised for the same reasons as the previous skill. There are three differences in execution: the angle of approach, the foot surface used and the area of the ball to be kicked. Paolo Rossi scores many goals with well-placed ground shots – the ability to bend the ball is clearly of immense value to him.

1 From a dead ball situation the angle of approach varies for the degree of spin required. For limited spin the approach will come from directly behind or just outside the line of the ball and its target. For extreme spin approach from a point further outside this line.

2 In order to keep the ball low it should be struck just above its horizontal mid-line surface. For extreme spin the outside surface to the back of the ball should be struck. For limited spin the ball should be struck along the extreme outside.

3 The surface area of the foot should be the outside area of the instep between the base of the little toe and the laces.

4 The standing foot should be behind the ball to allow the diagonal follow-through.

The Bent Volley (Inside Foot)

Steve Coppell *Manchester United and England*

Steve Coppell joined Manchester United in 1975 and was an 'ever-present' thereafter. He played as a winger with defensive responsibilities, and was particularly good at beating an opponent on the outside and crossing accurately from the goal-line. He was an intelligent player who scored many goals with his positional sense. He earned 42 caps, but unfortunately an injury in 1982 robbed England of his services in the World Cup finals, and a recurrence in 1983 forced him to give up football altogether.

The volley is a precise skill, particularly when swerve is added. The ball is struck while still in the air. The outside surface of the ball (i.e. the right-hand side for a right-foot volley) is struck with the upper inside surface of the instep to produce spin, causing the ball to follow a curve. This volley is hit with the body in an upright stance or with a slight leaning away from the ball. Steve Coppell with his immaculate control played some telling volleys.

1 When practising, the ball should be served from a throw so that it is descending at the time of impact to facilitate the straight stance. Fall-away techniques are usually applied to overcome the rising ball.

2 There are a number of adjustments that can be made to compensate for various heights of trajectories of the incoming ball. If the ball has dropped to a low level the leg can be fully extended at the time of impact. When the ball is high the upper leg needs to be flexed at the hip joint and the kicking action initiated at the knee joint.

3 The ball should be struck on the extreme outside. Where height and distance are required the ball should be struck on the underside with the foot following through. Where the ball is to be kept low it should be struck to the outside of the horizontal mid-line and the toes pointed downwards.

4 The upper inside area of the instep at the base of the big toe is the striking surface.

The Bent Volley (Outside Foot)

Luther Blissett *AC Milan and England*

Until AC Milan paid £1 million for him in 1983, Luther Blissett had been with Watford for the whole of his professional career, having come with them from the fourth division of the Football League to second place behind Liverpool in the first division. His first full appearance for England came in 1983 when he scored a hat-trick against Luxembourg. Previously he had played as a substitute against West Germany. In his last season with Watford he was the club's leading scorer with 26 goals.

This volley, as the previous one, is hit as the ball is in the air with the player in an upright position. The ball is hit with the outside of the foot. The skill is useful for delivering hard shots at goal as the ball passes across the player, and his fans can remember several Luther Blissett 'specials' delivered with this technique.

1 From a served ball which should be descending the player should allow sufficient distance between himself and the ball for the kicking action to be unfolded.

2 Repeat component (2) of previous skill.

3 The ball should be struck on the extreme inside. Where distance and height are required it should be struck on the outer underside. Where a direct trajectory is required the ball should be struck through the horizontal mid-line to the extreme outside.

4 The contact area of the foot is the outside of the foot at the base of the small toe.

5 For limited spin the foot will follow a straight line down the outside of the ball. For extreme spin it will follow a diagonal path, finishing to the outside of the standing foot.

John Barnes, in the colourful strip of Watford, gets up high to make a header against Birmingham.

Swerving Half-volley (Inside Foot)

Jesper Olsen *Denmark*

Jesper Olsen was the inspiration that took Denmark to the finals of the European Championship in 1984. Born in 1961, he is one of the brilliant young players who have transformed the Danish national team from one of the weaker sides of Europe to one that promises to be as good as that of Holland in the 1970s. He joined Naestved as a boy and was transferred to Ajax of Amsterdam when his ability became apparent. He can play in midfield, on the wing, or as an out-and-out striker, preferring to operate from the left. He scored a brilliant goal against England in 1983 to help Denmark top their European Championship group. He agreed to join Manchester United for the 1984-85 season.

This is a precise skill – if contact is not made with the ball as it strikes the ground, the effect will not be achieved and there is no recovery. Olsen has mastered this skill, which can produce goals when used when shooting, as his goal tally indicates. The ball must be struck through the extreme outside to produce spin (anti-clockwise when viewed from above from a right-foot volley).

1 You must position yourself for the moment when the ball hits the ground. The ball may come straight, or diagonally from either side, or even travel over you from behind: this skill is still practicable.

2 The great danger is overlift, so you must not be too far from the ball when it lands, or you must lean back and make contact with a fully extended leg. The standing foot can be behind the ball but not so far behind it as to make full leg extension necessary. The optimum position is with the toes of the standing foot alongside the back of the ball, with the knee over the ball and the foot pointed downwards.

3 The foot surface is the inside area of the instep at the base of the big toe.

4 The ball should be struck through the outside of the horizontal mid-line when the ball needs to be kept low, with the knee over the ball, and slightly beneath this point when height is required.

5 Greater spin can be produced by hitting the ball further round to the back.

Swerving Half-volley (Outside Foot)

Bernd Schuster *West Germany*

Bernd Schuster played for Cologne in West Germany but after he had played in West Germany's European Championship victory in 1980 he was bought by Barcelona for £800,000 to play in Spain. Schuster is a midfield general, an outspoken character who has differed with both his club manager, Udo Lattek, and the West German manager, Jupp Derwall. He did not play in the 1982 World Cup finals.

In this skill the ball must be struck as it hits the ground. It is struck on the inside (i.e. the opposite side to that struck in the previous skill). The outside of the upper foot between the laces and the base of the little toe is used. A midfield player like Schuster often finds himself in situations where a pass or clearance must be made on the half-volley and this technique is widely used.

1 You must position yourself for the moment when the ball hits the ground. The ball may come straight or diagonally from either side, or even travel over you from behind; this skill is still practicable.

2 The standing foot is behind the ball and the kicking foot addresses the extreme inside of the ball.

3 The foot surface is the outside of the upper foot between the laces and the base of the big toe.

4 If the ball is to be kept low the knee should be over the ball at the moment of impact.

5 Greater spin can be produced by hitting the ball further round to the back.

Scissors Overhead Kick

Zbigniew Boniek *Juventus and Poland*

Zbigniew Boniek first played as a professional for Widzew Lodz, although he did not receive money for playing, only 'material incentives'. He was soon in the first team and his first cap for Poland followed only a year later. He was one of Poland's best players in the 1978 World Cup in Argentina and was Poland's Footballer of the Year in both 1978 and 1979. He played well in the World Cup finals in 1982 in Spain, scoring a hat-trick against Belgium in the second-phase matches, but he was injured and could not play in the semi-final against Italy. His ambition was to play in West Germany, but despite an expressed dislike for English and Italian football he was signed by Juventus and now plays in Italy.

The scissors overhead kick is a spectacular skill which enables shots to be made when a player is facing his own goal and has no time or space to turn. The method may be expressed as getting the feet into the position occupied by the head. This is achieved by allowing the body to fall backwards, at the same time initiating a dynamic upward swing from the hip joint by the non-kicking leg. When the non-kicking leg is as high as the ball it is brought down with the kicking leg swinging up. The ball is kicked over the player's shoulder, which must be lower than the kicking foot. Boniek is a spectacular player who enjoys this skill.

1 You should be beneath the ball, with your back to the target. The legs should be bent at the knees ready for the upward thrust.

2 The jump is initiated off the non-kicking foot. The process of making the trunk fall away backwards and the upward launching of the non-kicking foot occur simultaneously. The fall back is delicate, while the upward thrust of the legs is dynamic. This results in the legs going slightly further than the horizontal point and the trunk staying slightly below it.

3 The mechanics of the kick will depend on the position of the body in relation to that of the ball. If, on reaching maximum height, the ball is still at a distance then the leg is extended and power is initiated from the hip.
If, however, the ball is close to the kicking foot flexion will take place at the knee, though power will still come from forward rotation at the hip joint.
Be careful how you fall!

Charlie Nicholas, Arsenal's expensive goal-scoring signing from Celtic.

Shot or Pass From Behind the Standing Foot

Gordon Cowans *Aston Villa*

Gordon Cowans had made 275 appearances for his club at 25 years of age. He had helped Aston Villa to become League champions, European champions and Super Cup winners. He was capped by England at under-21 and B level, and won his first full cap in 1982. A gifted, two-footed midfield player, he saw his career interrupted by a broken leg just before the 1983-84 season began, and the injury was very slow to heal.

This skill is designed to take opponents by surprise with its speed and unorthodoxy. With his two-footed control, Gordon Cowans can use it to catch markers on the wrong foot in the goal area. When a player is at the side of the ball he must jump off both feet, landing with the kicking foot having crossed behind the standing foot. By swinging at the knee, it is then brought into explosive contact with the ball. When the player is mobile the same action takes place.

1 Both feet need to be inside the ball if the line of the shot is straight: this is not necessary if the ball is to travel diagonally across the front of the player. The chest must face the target at the point of impact, whether the shot is diagonal or straight. The arms play a big part in swinging the trunk when the shot is diagonal.

2 For the straight shot the feet, before the jump, need to be level with the back end of the ball. The standing foot, however, needs to have its toes level with the far side of the ball at the moment of impact.
For the diagonal shot the standing foot can afford to be a couple of inches further back because the swivel compensates by allowing the kicking leg to come further round the standing leg, which swivels to point at the target.

3 Two surfaces are available and can be used to suit your position at the time of kicking. The toe can be used by driving it beneath the line of the ball. The alternative surface to this, if you have got near to the ball, is the instep surface close to the base of the toes. The toes should be on the ground at impact, bringing the instep higher up the ball.

Shoulder Shot or Pass

Norman Whiteside *Manchester United and Northern Ireland*

Norman Whiteside had a remarkable start to his career when he played for Manchester United at only 16 years of age, and with but two league appearances under his belt was chosen to lead the Northern Ireland attack in the World Cup in Spain in 1982. The youngest player in the tournament at 17, he played well in Northern Ireland's good run, and has since consolidated with some vital goals for Manchester United. He is a big strong forward, sometimes accused of being over-robust, but with plenty of skill allied to his strength.

This skill is not often seen, which is surprising in view of its power and deceptiveness. It is a useful skill for a player to have when the ball is travelling towards him at speed and at a height where control is difficult. It is especially attractive to a powerful player like Norman Whiteside.

1 You should be chest-on to the oncoming ball. The feet should be apart to aid balance. Preceding impact, the striking shoulder is withdrawn away from the ball before being thrust forward with as much speed as possible.

2 The bony area at the front of the shoulder is the contact surface.

3 The ball should be struck through the horizontal and vertical mid-lines of the ball.

4 The shoulder can be used to lob the ball at the same time as propelling it forward by combining an upward movement with the forward movement, thereby getting height as well as distance. The shoulder can be used for juggling the ball as a specific skill or incorporated in an integrated routine. (See Skill number 23 in the juggling section.)

The Back Spin Chip

Giancarlo Antognoni *Italy*

Giancarlo Antognoni is a brilliant midfield player for Florence and Italy, who orchestrates the rhythm of the Italian national side when it is on song. Much of the early success of Paolo Rossi was owed to the perception and guile of Antognoni's prompting. Born on April Fool's Day 1954, he first played for Italy when only 20, but his career has often been dogged by injury. He fractured his skull in the season before the 1982 World Cup, but nevertheless returned to play brilliantly in Spain, although injury again forced him to miss the Final.

This chip is used when early height is needed to pass the ball over the head of an opponent who is close. Back spin helps, and also slows the ball when it lands. The foot strikes beneath the ball, without the follow-through needed for a drive. When Antognoni uses this skill, a great deal of elevation comes from flexion taking place at the hip joint at the moment of impact, leaving the thigh in a horizontal position (i.e. the knee is not straightened).

1 Approach can be direct or angled Here we are dealing with the direct approach.

2 The standing foot is placed to the side of and behind the ball.

3 The kicking foot stabs beneath the ball with the toes and base of the instep.

4 Using the Antognoni technique, the skill is viable even where the ground is hard. When the toes and then the instep are beneath the ball the leg remains bent at the knee, with the leg completing a half-circle of backward rotation at the hip.

5 Where distance is required, straightening at the knee will be necessary, but on dry ground this will be at the expense of height.

Heel Pass at Right Angles to Player's Run

Craig Johnston *Liverpool*

Craig Johnston plays for England, but was born in South Africa of Scottish parentage and grew up in Australia. His first game for Liverpool after joining them from Middlesborough for £500,000 in 1981 was unfortunate, as the European Champions lost 3-0 to Flamengo in the World Club Championship in Tokyo. Johnston is an attacking midfield player, with the talent to score important goals.

This skill is excellent for switching play, preserving the element of disguise up to the last moment. With the correct technique a square pass can be struck with the heel at right angles to the player's progress. A direct running player like Craig Johnston will often find an opponent blocking his path, but with a square pass to a colleague 'on', and this technique will deliver the pass without the defence anticipating it.

1 If you are making a straight run for the opponent's goal you may see the opportunity or necessity for a square pass.

2 For the sake of total deception, if you are playing the ball with the outside of your foot and moving away from the direction of the intended pass, the playing foot must be switched from being turned inwards to being turned outwards, at right angles to the other foot. It is the brought across in a swinging action initiated at the knee, causing the ball to travel across the standing foot.

3 If the ball is to be kept low and the pass is fairly long, the horizontal and vertical mid-lines should be aimed for.

Half-volley Heel Shot or Pass

Gary Stevens *Spurs*

Gary Stevens was born in Suffolk, and was rejected by Ipswich Town who had some good centre backs on their books like England's Terry Butcher and Russell Osman. Stevens signed for Alan Mullery at Brighton and established himself in the first team. His excellent performances in the 1983 FA Cup Final against Manchester United led to him being voted 'man of the match' by TV audiences and critics. He was shortly afterwards signed by Tottenham Hotspur. An Under-21 international, he is bidding strongly for full England honours.

The skill is best used when the player is facing away from the target and the ball is approaching his back or dropping vertically. The precise timing of a Gary Stevens is required to contact the ball at the same time as the ball touches the ground.

1 When the ball is approaching from behind and there is no time to turn, the kicking leg is flexed at the knee ready for the ball's arrival.

2 The thigh is lifted slightly and the leg bent at the knee. The kicking leg sweeps across the standing leg, leverage taking place at the knee and striking with the heel through the horizontal mid-line of the ball.

Gary Stevens, signed by Spurs after an excellent display in the FA Cup Final for Brighton.

Reverse Side Control and Reverse Side Pass

Ricky Hill *Luton Town*

Ricky Hill made his debut for Luton Town in the second division in 1976 and quickly matured into an extremely influential midfield member of the side. Luton gained promotion to the first division in 1981-82 and Hill was the first new player capped by Bobby Robson when he took over the England management after the 1982 World Cup.

In this skill, when the ball is travelling to the left side of the player, he crosses his right foot over to control with the outside area of the instep, bringing the ball across to a position outside the natural position of the right foot. He then crosses the left foot over and strikes the ball with the outside of the instep, returning the ball in the direction whence it came. Thus, if the ball is travelling to the player's left, the controlling foot is the right, and the kicking foot the left. This is reversed, of course, when the ball is travelling to the right. It is a two-touch skill which Ricky Hill uses to deceive a close marker.

1 When the ball approaches to your left side, the right foot should cross over in front of the left foot to take the pass with the outside surface of the foot, at the base of the little toe.

2 The ball should be swept across to your right-hand side in the same movement as taking pace off the pass, which is achieved by extending the controlling foot to the ball and withdrawing it on impact.

3 When the ball has been transferred to the right side the left foot is crossed over with the foot turned in. The ball is then struck with the outside instep in the direction it came from.

The Thigh Shot or Pass

Trevor Brooking *West Ham United*

Trevor Brooking joined West Ham straight from school in 1965 and has been a faithful one-club man ever since. An elegant and constructive attacking midfield player, who likes to raid down the wings, he was first picked for England in 1974 and has appeared nearly 50 times since. He was injured before the 1982 World Cup, but was brought on as a substitute in the final game and immediately nearly broke the deadlock with a near-miss against Spain. He is not principally a goal-scorer, but in around 700 appearances for West Ham has scored over 100 goals, including the only goal in the 1980 FA Cup Final, and his goals for England include two in Hungary which were vital for England to qualify for the World Cup finals.

A thigh shot or pass cannot be compared in efficiency or power with the range of shots or passes using the feet, but on those occasions when waiting for the ball to reach the foot means a probable loss of possession or opportunity, then the thigh can be used with advantage. Trevor Brooking is a master opportunist in tight situations. The ball is struck with the thigh when it has dropped to a point beneath the hips (if the ball is above this point it is lobbed). This allows the thigh to be midway between the straight and horizontal position at the time of contact.

1 Get beneath, and where possible in line with, the flight path of the ball.

2 Where the ball comes in from the side and the shot is to be made in a forward direction you should face the ball. The thigh is raised and brought across the standing leg with sideways rotation at the hip.

3 If the ball is played with the thigh at or above the horizontal position it will rise vertically. The ball should be allowed to fall beneath the hips so that contact can be made with the thigh between the straight and horizontal position.

4 Where the angle of the shot differs from the angle of the incoming ball, at the point of impact the player pivots on the standing foot, so that when the skill is completed he is facing the target.

Sling Shot or Pass from Caught Ball

François van der Elst *Belgium*

François van der Elst first attracted the attention of West Ham United when he scored two goals against them for Anderlecht in the European Cup Winners Cup Final in 1976. Later he was in the side that beat Liverpool in the Super Cup in 1978. A Belgian international midfielder, he played in the 1982 World Cup finals in Spain.

The first part of this skill is the top foot catch (the skill of Ramon Diaz, described in the Basic Control Techniques section). For the van der Elst addition, the sling shot or pass, the ball is best controlled from a short drop, e.g. off the thigh (as described in the Willy Miller skill, also in the Basic Control Techniques section). Once the ball is caught, the leg is withdrawn, still clasping the ball, and thrust forward explosively, releasing the ball before the forward action has expired.

1 The ball should be caught in the manner described in the Basic Control Techniques section (the skill of Ramon Diaz).

2 With the ball clasped between the upper surface of the toes and the shin, it is held with the thigh just below the horizontal point. The leg is drawn back, straightening the thigh.

3 The foot is then thrust forward explosively with leverage at the knee.

4 Just before release the foot is pointed and the ball rolled to the upper toe surface. This gives the shot trajectory and extra power.

Passing with the Outside of Either Foot

John Barnes *Watford*

John Barnes was born in Jamaica, forced himself into the Watford side, and in his first full season (1981-82) scored 13 goals as Watford gained promotion to the first division. Next season Watford were first division runners-up and Barnes' performances earned him his first England cap. A direct winger, usually on the right, he has a good first touch and knows the way to goal. When Luther Blissett left Watford for AC Milan before the 1983-84 season Barnes played a more central attacking role with great success.

Controlling the ball with the outside surface of the foot is superior in important ways to control with the inside of the foot. It enables the ball to be taken further from an opponent, and it helps mobility for subsequent moves. This skill provides good exercise for developing co-ordination. If the ball comes to the player's left the pass is returned by the outside surface of the right foot and vice versa. It is a useful skill which John Barnes takes full advantage of, as it enables him to make a first-time return pass while retaining balance and mobility for a quick run.

1 Have a partner to serve the ball to you at medium pace or play the ball off a wall.

2 When the ball approaches to your left side the right foot should cross over to return the pass with the outside surface of the foot at the base of the little toe.

3 When the ball comes to your right side the left foot should cross over to return the pass with the outside surface as described in (2).

4 At the time of passing the body is slightly diagonal to the intended line of the pass.

5 There is very little follow through in the kicking action.

The Inside Foot Flick

George Best

It was the tragedy of George Best that Northern Ireland could not reach the World Cup finals while Best was at his prime, so that his dazzling skills were not paraded on the world stage. Nevertheless many observers claim that Best was the only player in the last two decades who could possibly have challenged Pelé for the title 'King of Soccer'. Like Pelé, Best shone at every aspect of the game. Apart from his 37 caps for Northern Ireland, his triumphs were for Manchester United. A brilliant dribbler who mainly operated on the wings, Best could also score with head or foot and registered many outstanding individual goals, one of the best remembered being that which put Manchester United in the lead and on the way to victory in the European Cup Final against Benfica in 1968.

This skill requires great flexibility at the ankle and knee joints. The player usually has his back to the target and legs slightly apart. The ball is flicked with the inside of the foot so that the ball passes behind the standing foot. It is a good skill for making a return pass for a colleague to run on to. It was only one of the many techniques in George Best's repertoire.

1 Face the ball with the back to the target.

2 As the ball draws level with the controlling foot it is flicked behind the standing foot with a whiplash action which emanates from the ankle and knee joints.

3 The playing surface is the inside of the foot at the base of the big toe.

4 For the ball to travel diagonally the standing foot needs to be slightly forward of the playing foot.

The Scissors Pass

Garth Crooks *Tottenham Hotspur*

After impressing with Stoke City, Garth Crooks was signed by Spurs during the 1980 close season for a fee of £800,000. He scored 22 goals in his first season with Spurs, including an equalizer in the FA Cup Final of 1981, and was the club's top scorer with 18 in the following season. A fast and mobile striker, Crooks has played for England B and Under-21 sides. He makes himself a target man for colleagues to send him on fast and penetrating runs deep into the opposing defence.

This skill is a dynamic version of the previous skill, ideal for returning diagonal passes on the blind side of opponents. The legs cross over, with the playing foot behind the standing foot. Both legs are kept straight throughout the skill and good timing is essential. A fast player like Crooks can play this ball and make a run at right angles to the pass before the defence can realize what is happening.

1 Face the pass with your body sideways on to the intended direction of the pass.

2 Just before the ball arrives make a one-footed jump off the standing foot, lifting the playing foot and keeping both legs straight.

3 The ball is played with the inside surface bringing the ball across and behind the standing foot.

4 At the end of the pass the legs should be crossed, with the playing leg behind the standing leg.

Heel Shot or Pass after Running Beneath the Ball

Paolo Roberto Falcao *Roma and Brazil*

The fair-haired midfield player Falcao was outstanding in the 1982 World Cup Finals in Spain, where he played brilliantly in the artistic Brazilian side. He began with Internacional of Porte Alegre, and after helping his side to three Brazilian titles he joined Roma in 1980, helping them to an Italian championship win in 1982-83. Aged 30, he has 27 caps for Brazil.

This skill is useful when running beneath a bouncing ball and arriving too early to make a shot. With an explosive flexing of the knee towards the player's rear he hits the ball with his heel. A player may have the audacity to try this as a premeditated ploy, deliberately arriving too early for a header and surprising the opposition with this shot or pass. It requires the confidence and skill of a Falcao to forego the header and use the heel.

1 You need to run in so that the descending ball is slightly to the outside of the playing foot.

2 Timing is essential. Having run beneath the ball the playing leg, which is the trailing leg, is fully flexed at the knee in the position a hurdler's trailing leg would occupy as he cleared the hurdle.

3 You must incline your trunk forward to get height for the back leg.

4 The combination of obtaining maximum flexion at the knee, your forward momentum, and the tilt of the trunk, all combine to produce a very powerful shot.

5 The lower leg is angled to be outside the line of the upper leg at the point of contact so as to give clearance along the outside of your body.

6 The point between the rear of the ankle and the heel is the striking surface.

The Chest Pass

Cyril Regis *West Bromwich Albion*

Cyril Regis is a big strong central attacker who has made over 200 appearances for his club since joining them in 1977 for a fee of only £5000. He was discovered playing non-league football for Hayes in Middlesex. Powerful with head and foot, he has scored over 70 goals for his club. After progressing through the England B and Under-21 sides he was given his first full cap in 1982.

This skill is ideal for taking pace from a ball which arrives at medium height and passing it over a short distance with control and the pace absorbed. A strong player with a big chest like Regis can play this first-time pass with accuracy.

1 Try to get square on to the incoming ball.

2 The chest is not extended to the ball.

3 When the ball arrives to the chest, extension then takes place causing the ball to travel forward off the chest.

4 The pass often has to be made at a different angle to the incoming pass and the movement for reducing the pace stems from the hips with movement of the trunk, rotating at the hips, in the direction of the pass.

5 The pass is more effective when the ball is directed downwards. The mechanics of this are described in the Basic Skill Technique of Tony Woodcock (the concave chest trap).

Juggling Skills

This section of the book differs from preceding sections. The skills here are not specific tricks or techniques to use in various situations in a match. They are rather presented as exercises designed to improve a player's control of the ball. They increase the options of the player presented with a ball in the air, and they increase the ways in which he can get the ball from the ground to the air. Also, whereas the skills in the previous sections are self-contained and not offered in any particular order, these juggling skills are presented as a progressive programme from which the player will best benefit by working through them in the numbered order.

They are enjoyable exercises and a legitimate part of the day's training programme for any developing player. It is not suggested that the game of football itself should be characterized by the inclusion of constant juggling exhibitions. But practising these skills will improve a player's confidence with the ball, and there is no reason why a player with sufficient audacity shouldn't be able to use them to advantage in a match.

(Left) *Zico of Brazil makes his header before Passarella of Argentina can challenge in the World Cup match.*

(1) Flick Up From Sole-roll

This is the most common method of getting the ball into the air, especially for a juggling movement.

The ball is pulled towards the player with the ball of the foot immediately on top of the ball. The sole rolls down the ball, spinning the ball backwards. At the point where the toe has finally left the ball's surface it is dug beneath the spinning ball and levered upwards, launching the ball into flight.

1 Pull ball back by the sole of the foot, which is placed on the top of the ball.

2 Flex the leg at the hip. Once the ball has been pulled back, flexion takes place at the knee.

3 Lift the ball by the upper foot surface.

4 The movement comes from backward rotation of the hip, although the knee is still bent.

(2) Two-footed Pincer Flick

This skill is designed to get the ball off the ground, keeping it close to the controlling player. The feet are placed either side of the ball and pointing outwards diagonally. They are snapped together swiftly, causing the ball to rise upwards to about knee level.

1 Place the feet each side of the ball with the centre of the ball level with the inside base of each big toe. The toes should be pointed diagonally outwards.

2 The soles should be slightly raised off the ground, throwing all the weight on to the heels.

3 Snap the toes together in a fast powerful action beneath the ball, with swivel taking place on the heels.

4 The ball will rise vertically upwards towards the knee cap and should be redirected by the upper foot to the next surface.

(3) One-foot Juggle From Flick-up

For those learning the skill of juggling, confidence is best gained and rhythm mastered by perfecting the art with one's natural foot. In this combination the ball is flicked up as described in Juggling Skill 1 and then juggled using the one foot, attempting a maximum number of consecutive touches without the ball touching the ground.

1 Flick up as in Juggling Skill 1.

2 Keep the ball airborne by keeping the foot at right angles to the leg, thereby making a platform for the ball to hit.

3 The juggling leg should be bent at the knee and the ball kept close to the foot.

4 The number of touches without the playing foot touching the ground should be as few as possible, since this places great strain on the player's balance.

5 Where the ball is played too high or deflected at a bad angle the skill should be started again rather than having the player struggle to reassert control.

(4) Two-footed Juggle from Flick-up

Progress to the use of two feet in keeping continuous aerial control should only be made when some rhythm and balance with a player's best foot have been established. The same principles of leg position and foot surface apply. As an aid to negotiating the transfer from one foot to another, neither the receiving foot nor the ball wants to be too high. This cuts down the risk of unwanted deflections and impaired balance.

1 Flick up as in Juggling Skill 1.

2 With flexion at the hip and knee joint and the foot held horizontally, balance and rhythm should be established with the good foot.

3 The transfer to the other foot should be effected not with a vertical ball but with a ball which is looped so as to fall vertically on to the other foot. Where this is not achieved body movement should take place so as to position the receiving foot beneath the dropping ball.

4 When confidence is gained the ball should be hit at varying heights and at varying speeds.

(5) One-foot Catch Juggle

This juggle can be started in any way, i.e. from a ball bounced, thrown or flicked up. The ball is caught between the upper surface of the toes and the shin in a pincer action. The foot should be taken up to meet the dropping ball and relaxed at the moment of impact so as to ride with the ball. The ball having been caught, it is thrown up by the holding foot and the movement is repeated.

1 (Starting from flick-up). Flick the ball up as in Juggling Skill 1 until poise and balance are established.

2 At the optimum moment catch the ball as described in the skill 'Top Foot Catch' (the Ramon Diaz skill in the 'Basic Control Techniques' section).

3 The controlling foot is lifted upwards at the hip joint and the ball released from the pincer movement at the beginning of the upward stroke.

4 The controlling foot is raised to the descending ball and relaxes on impact so that the second catch can be effected.

5 These actions are repeated for as many catches as the player can make, always trying to beat his previous best score.

6 Beware of balancing for too long on the standing foot alone. Try to make regular touch downs with the controlling foot to assist stability.

Tony Woodcock with the ball under control for England.

(6) Two-footed Catch Juggle

The mechanics described previously for the one-foot catch juggle apply for this skill almost exactly, the exception being the transfer from one side of the body to the other. This is the most difficult component. To catch a ball in this way when it is travelling from the side is extremely hard. Therefore, when the ball is thrown upwards from one foot, it has also to be looped so as to fall directly to the new receiving foot.

1 As in Juggling Skill 5.

2 As in Juggling Skill 5.

3 As in Juggling Skill 5.

4 So that the ball drops directly for the new

controlling foot it must be thrown upwards and across in a looping movement.

5 The receiving foot must be raised towards the transferred ball and relaxed on impact.

(7) Top-foot Catch and Carry

The top-foot catch has been described, and comprises the first part of this skill. When the ball has been securely caught between the upper surface of the toes and the shin, the player hops forward on the standing foot, still clutching the ball. This skill will rarely be used in a competitive game, but is very useful for football tennis, squash, etc.

1 Catch the ball as described in the skill 'Top Foot Catch' (the Ramon Diaz skill in the 'Basic Control Techniques' section).

2 The leg should be flexed at the knee with the thigh just below horizontal.

3 The player hops forward on the standing leg holding the ball in a top-foot catch.

4 The player can hop backwards with the ball in a top-foot catch.

(8) The Shovel Lift

Different kinds of kicking technique produce different rates of ascent, when we are kicking for height and where the ball is on the ground. The drive, for example, will rise more slowly than the chip. This skill is designed to bring about steep and immediate ascent from a dead ball situation or one in which the ball is moving away from the player.

1 The standing foot should be alongside the ball.

2 The playing foot should be placed beneath the ball. This is the component that distinguishes this skill from other kicking skills. The foot can approach the ball at speed but must be slowed down just before impact to prevent the ball being knocked forward.

3 Once the toes are beneath the ball rotation at the hip and flexion at the knee will cause the ball to rise immediately.

4 When the ball has left the playing foot, the thighs should be in a horizontal position.

5 Forward movement of the ball can be achieved by straightening the leg.

(9) Thigh Juggle

In this juggling skill, a ball tossed into the air by the player is played off the fleshy part of the thigh. Because the thigh is an absorbent surface the ball can be bounced quite high, giving more time for correct position.

1 Throw the ball into the air just above the head. Bring the thigh upwards to the horizontal position to make contact with the ball.

2 After each touch a natural standing position should be assumed and the thigh brought up to the horizontal position to make contact with the ball.

3 If the ball is played too early it will result in the ball coming back to the player's chest; if the ball is played too late it will bounce away from the player. Therefore the horizontal position of the thigh is the one to be aimed at.

4 As the player becomes more adept so the pace and height of balls played off the thigh should be varied.

(10) Upper Foot and Thigh Combination Juggle

This combination can be started from a dropped ball on to the thigh or from a flick-up on to the upper foot. Both skills have been dealt with individually. The important factor in this skill is that of transfer from one surface to the other. The player should, at first, attempt to get transfer from one surface to the other when the time is right, rather than follow a predetermined sequence.

1 Flick-up as in Juggling Skill 1.

2 The ball is played on the upper foot as in Juggling Skill 3.

3 The transfer from the foot to the thigh is best effected with flexion at the knee so that the ball follows a straight vertical line.

4 Ensure that the receiving surface (the thigh) is placed directly beneath the dropping ball.

5 The transfer from the thigh to the upper foot should be effected with a minimum of height off the thigh so as to make control easier for the upper foot.

(11) Thigh and Foot Catch Juggle

When attempting to catch a dropping ball on the upper foot it is often best to break the rate of descent of the ball with the thigh. In this combination skill the ball is passed from the thigh in a bounce, to be caught on the upper foot, balanced, then returned.

1 The use of the thigh surface has been comprehensively dealt with in this section and the mechanics so far described apply to this skill.

2 A relaxed and well-balanced thigh juggle should be set in motion, ensuring that the controlling foot returns to the ground as often as possible.

3 The ball should be dropped from the thigh, taking care not to produce too much height since this will make the catch more difficult.

4 The catching foot should be brought up to the ball and relaxed on impact, when the pincer movement between the toes and the shin should be applied.

5 The ball should be held in this position and then thrown back up to the thigh.

(12) Juggle Spin

This skill is ideally suited to control a ball which is descending but has a fairly direct trajectory. It is also a useful way of defusing the ball when the player is moving backwards. The pace is taken off the ball by applying backspin to the underside and rolling the ball backwards in this fashion.

1 Line the chest up to the flight path of the ball.

2 Do not raise the playing foot any more than 30 cm (1 ft) off the ground, as this will restrict the movement required to produce the backspin. The leg should swing from the knee, with the upper foot playing the underside of the ball.

3 The arms play an important part in maintaining balance

and should be spread wide. The player may be hopping backwards as he performs the skill, so good balance is a critical feature.

4 The part of the foot at the base of the toes and the bottom of the instep is the controlling surface. This forms a cradle for the secure rotation of the ball. This skill is an ideal forerunner to the volley, the half volley or the lob.

(13) Sequence Juggles

Sequence Juggling is where predetermined surfaces and numbers of touches are nominated before the performance of the routine. This is excellent training and discipline for controlling pace, direction and mental alertness.

1 Begin by naming surfaces at which you know you are proficient, e.g. two touches right upper foot, two touches right thigh, two touches left thigh.

2 Rotate these surfaces in this order until you have mastered the technique of transfer between them with fluency.

3 Surfaces with which you are not so proficient should be in the minority in any sequence until they become fully co-ordinated skills.

4 The target should be to combine surfaces in sequence which are furthest away from each other, e.g. right upper foot (two touches) to head (two touches) to left upper foot (two touches) to shoulder (two touches).

5 Further physical co-ordination and mental alertness are developed by varying the number of touches at each surface.

Ossie Ardiles of Argentina takes the ball away from Serginho of Brazil in the 1982 World Cup.

(14) Using the Shoulder with Other Juggling Surfaces

In this juggling section we have described how to use the upper foot, thigh, chest and head as well as the shoulder to keep the ball in flight and under control. It is best at first not to decide which particular surfaces are to be used but to play to those surfaces which are appropriate to the position of the ball at the time of transfer. The step-by-step section shows a selection of surfaces as a suggestion rather than an inflexible sequence.

1 All the components for this combination are to be found elsewhere in the juggling section. There are certain demands imposed by transfer between the surfaces which will be thought of now as components.

2 Transfer from upper foot to shoulder requires sufficient height for the ball to drop directly on to the playing surface.

3 Transfer from thigh to shoulder must have the same height and descent patterns as for the upper foot.

(15) Mobile One-footed Juggle

Juggling with the upper foot is the most popular form of exploratory soccer practised today, primarily because it is the easiest and most straightforward. It is surprising, nonetheless, how many players cannot master the rhythm and co-ordination essential for this skill, especially when mobility is required. The idea is to keep the ball in the air, using the upper foot at the same time as moving forward.

1 Start from a bounced ball rather than a dropped ball. This will make initial control easier.

2 The foot is held in the horizontal position while the leg is slightly flexed at the knee.

3 Control is made easier if the ball is not played too high.

4 Forward movement initially should be restrained to a walk and gradually speeded up as the technique is mastered.

5 Return the kicking foot to the ground after each touch.

6 Never try to recover badly struck balls – start again.

7 Keep a score of the number of touches made without the ball touching the ground so that progress can be measured.

(16) Two-Footed Mobile Juggle

This is the logical progression from the previous skill. The components described there apply here. There is added difficulty in this skill caused by the transfer of the ball from one foot to the other and also by the use of the weaker foot.

1 A reasonable standard of proficiency will have been reached in the previous skill before proceeding to this one; therefore the juggle can be started from a flick-up or a dropped ball.

2 The ball should be transferred from one side to the other in a diagonal loop, enabling forward progress to be made at the same time as allowing the ball to drop on to the other foot.

3 The lower the ball is kept the more touches there will be over a given period, but the higher a ball is played the more difficult will be control at each touch.

4 Back spin is a useful application in this skill, to keep the ball rotating back towards the player as he progresses, and in slowing the aerial flight of the ball.

Variations
1 Using back spin try to make progress while keeping the ball within 5-8 cm (2-3 in) of the upper foot surface being used.

2 Using back spin see how far you can get running backwards and juggling the ball at the same time.

(17) Mobile Thigh Juggle

The skill description used for the previous juggle applies to this skill except that the ball comes off the thigh slightly forward of vertical and the lean-back is emphasized.

1 To make the ball bounce slightly forward of the vertical position contact has to be made before the thigh reaches a horizontal plane.

2 After each contact the player moves forward to arrive with the thigh beneath the descending ball.

Variations
1 Greater control can be developed by following predetermined sequences: two touches left thigh, one tough right thigh, one touch left thigh, two touches right thigh.

2 Skill and sensitivity in putting the right weight on the ball can be achieved by varying the height of each bounce. This can also be put into a sequence independent of the previous sequence or linked to it.

3 Knock the ball high and well forward, spring to get beneath it with the thigh surface and control.

Steve Archibald of Spurs protects the ball from Ian Gillard of QPR in the 1982 FA Cup Final.

(18) Mobile Juggle Using All Surfaces

The pinnacle of the juggling repertoire and only for those who have worked at and accomplished the various components which precede it. The routine can be performed stationary but is best set to a particular distance, e.g. using all surfaces over a distance of 50 metres. All surfaces means upper foot, thigh, chest, each shoulder and head, and the whole routine can be rounded off with a catch trap.

Begin by flicking the ball up with the sole roll. The accompanying photographs show the sequence of components from flick-up to catch trap.

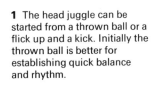

(19) Head Juggle

Controlled heading develops the player's ability to understand pace, timing and direction as well as his capacity to cope with the vertically descending ball.

1 The head juggle can be started from a thrown ball or a flick up and a kick. Initially the thrown ball is better for establishing quick balance and rhythm.

2 The head should be angled backwards so that the forehead is presented as a platform to the dropping ball.

3 The player must keep his eyes on the ball at all times and keep his head directly beneath the line of descent.

4 For this skill power is generated by flexion at the knee joints causing upward movement of the whole body beneath the ball.

5 As an aid to getting a 'feel' for the pace of the ball the player should vary the distance of each header, heading both for height and close control.

6 Try heading the ball in this way at the same time as moving towards a target.

7 Try heading for distance, sprinting to the dropping ball, and controlling with the head.

(20) Head and Shoulder Juggle

The shoulder being a bony surface is not an ideal juggling platform. For this reason subtlety of touch needs to be developed. Experiment at first by dropping the ball towards the shoulder, dipping the opposite shoulder down, while bending at the hips. Providing no swivel has taken place at the hip the ball should pass over the head from side to side, i.e. towards the other shoulder. By repeating the motion in the opposite direction it will be possible to loop the ball to and fro between the two shoulders. The introduction of the head as an intermediary surface demands a more sensitive contact at the shoulders and greater co-ordination.

1 From a ball thrown just above the head the shoulder must be placed just beneath the line of descent.

2 Experimentation must take place as to the height produced by different degrees of dipping the opposite shoulder.

3 Beware of producing swivel at the hips as this will send the ball forward rather than directly over or on to the player's head.

4 Once a rhythm is established between the shoulders the head can be introduced by directing the ball from the shoulder to the forehead.

(21) Two-footed Flick Up Using Heels

In this juggling skill the ball needs to be static or moving slowly. The player traps the ball between his heels and, by throwing the legs backwards and upwards and releasing the ball when the lower legs have formed a V with the upper legs, the ball is thrown over the player's head.

1 From a one-footed take-off make a two-footed landing with one foot placed on each side of the ball.

2 The inside instep towards the heels is clamped to each side of the ball.

3 The lower legs are now thrown upwards and backwards, lifting the ball between the feet.

4 When the lower legs form a V with the upper legs the ball should be released to travel over the player's head.

5 If the ball is released too early it is thrown out backwards. If it is released too late it hits the player's back.

(22) Flick Up Between Heel and Top Foot

There are many ways of getting a dead ball into the air, and the pull and flick up have already been discussed. This method is a more complex skill demanding greater co-ordination, but mastery of it will produce great satisfaction. The ball is trapped between the upper toes and instep of the back foot against the heel and Achilles tendon of the front foot. The front foot then flicks the ball up, to the back of the player and over his head.

1 The ball can be still or rolling away from the player. Most players like to put their best foot forward but this is up to the individual.

2 Place the front foot in front of the ball.

3 As the heel of the front foot makes contact with the ball the upper toes and instep of the trailing foot must close with the back of the ball, trapping it against the heel.

4 The front leg must now be flexed explosively towards the player's rear. He will have both feet off the ground at this stage.

5 The back foot only releases contact with the ball once movement (4) has been initiated.

6 If the ball does not come over the player it could be due to two factors:
(a) the ball is not being rolled high enough up the back of the front leg;
(b) flexion at the knees is not fast enough.

(23) Head Catch and Neck Trap

The idea of this skill is to catch the ball on the forehead. As with the catch trap the playing surface is extended towards the ball and relaxed on impact. Invariably because of the hardness of the surface several touches are required to absorb the pace before the ball is finally rested on the forehead. Forward and downward movement of the head will cause the ball to roll over the back of the head. The ball is then caught in the cradle formed between the base of the head and the nape of the neck.

1 From a thrown ball the forehead surface should be relaxed on impact so as to absorb the pace. Several touches may be required to completely 'defuse' the ball.

2 The ball should be balanced on the forehead until it is still.

3 Foreward rotation of the head now takes place taking the chin down to the chest, causing the ball to roll over the back of the head; the chin is then thrust forward, the shoulders snapped back and the trunk bent forwards at the hips, to form a cradle between the top of the spine and the nape of the neck, in which the ball can rest.

Variation
1 The ball can then be rolled down the back and kicked with the back of the heel over the player's head to his front.

Kenny Dalglish, Liverpool and Scotland, with the ball on his toe.

Units of Skill Development

These exercises form a graded scheme of advancement through the skills shown in this book, based upon the degree of difficulty, as judged by the author during an experience of coaching a wide range of pupils.

The early steps, which form the first part of this section, use those skills which are closest to the basics, but with small variations which raise them from the level of repetitive practice to the stage of early exploration. They form an appropriate link between the basic fundamental skills and the more sophisticated skills of the advanced steps which follow in the second part of this section.

The skills in each step should be worked at individually on a regular basis until a high degree of proficiency is attained. The next stage is to merge the skills in the order in which they are shown in each step into a fluent routine, one skill flowing smoothly into the next.

Free flow work, where skills are produced naturally to cope with each new situation, will obviously follow when a wide range of techniques have been mastered. Instinctive reactions to situations which arise in a match will follow more readily when a player has a variety of techniques at his disposal. In the formative stage, however, artificial situations, such as practising a predetermined programme of skills, are an essential discipline if a young player is to progress logically to an all-round proficiency.

The advanced steps which form the second part of this section have much the same pattern, in that progress is schematic and linked to gradual increases in the degree of difficulty. The complexity of each skill is increased and consequently the transition from one skill to the other is more demanding.

Early steps in skill development

The five sequences which follow are based on the basic skills described in the four previous sections: Dribbling Skills; Basic Control Techniques; Shooting and Passing; and Juggling Skills.

Certain of these skills have been put together to form the sequences. It is assumed that the reader will have worked on these skills individually and attained a standard of efficiency in each.

By now practising the skills in the various sequences, the player will bring added interest to his practice sessions and develop a skill and confidence in putting together his techniques in a natural, flowing and consequently effective manner.

1

1 Run with the ball using the inside of one foot.

2 Stop the ball with the sole of the foot. See Dribbling Skills: *Sole of the Foot Control* (Paul Mariner).

3 Pull the ball back in the opposite direction. See Dribbling Skills: *The Backward Toe Roll* (Bruno Conti).

4 Dribble, using the outside surface of one foot. See Dribbling Skills: *Dribbling Using Both Outside Foot Surfaces* (Mark Barham).

5 Flick-up from sole roll and bend a half-volley at a large target with the inside instep. See Shooting and Passing: *Swerving the Half-volley (Inside Foot)* (Jesper Olsen).

2

1 From a bounced ball, make four top-foot touches without the ball hitting the ground. See Juggling Skills No. 3.

2 Perform a two-footed juggle. Six touches, three each foot. See Juggling Skill No. 4.

3 From a dropped ball, control with a top foot pace absorber. See Basic Control Techniques: *The Top Foot Pace Absorber* (Socrates).

4 Perform *The Step-over* dummy over a 15-metre dribbling run. See Dribbling Skill: *The Step-over* (Eder).

5 Perform a backward toe-roll over 15 metres. See Dribbling Skills: *The Backward Toe Roll* (Bruno Conti).

3

1 Kick the ball high and control with a thigh trap. See Basic Control Techniques: *The Thigh Bounce* (Mario Tardelli).

2 Perform three top-foot touches on each foot. See Juggling Skill No. 4.

3 From high ball, control with the head and juggle three times on the head. See Juggling Skill No. 19.

4 Make a cross-legged outside foot trap from dropped ball. See Basic Control Techniques: *Cross-legged Outside Foot Trap* (Ray Wilkins).

5 Perform one reverse step-over over a 15-metre run. See Dribbling Skills: *The Reverse Step-over* (Mark Chamberlain).

4

1 From a ball rolled along the ground at medium pace use the inside foot ride. Basic Control Techniques: *The Inside Foot Ride* (Alan Sunderland).

2 Perform a sole of the foot control, pulling the ball in three different angles. See Dribbling Skills: *Sole of the Foot Control* (Paul Mariner).

3 Stop the ball with the sole using two-footed pincer movement. See Juggling Skill No. 2.

4 Kick the ball above the head and control with a convex chest trap. See Basic Control Techniques: *The Convex Chest Trap with Ball Rolling Down Body* (Michel Platini).

5 From previous skill use top foot pace absorber. See Basic Control Techniques: *The Top Foot Pace Absorber* (Socrates).

5

1. From a thrown ball use a convex chest trap, to thigh, to top foot catch. See Basic Control Techniques: *Convex Chest Trap with Ball Rolling Down Body* (Michel Platini); *The Thigh Bounce* (Marco Tardelli); *The Top Foot Catch* (Ramon Diaz).

2 Run with the ball over 30 metres using sole roll technique. See Dribbling Skills: *The Cross Pull* (Zico), component four.

3 Return, using the sole roll technique. See Dribbling Skills: *The Cross Pull* (as above).

4 Flick-up from sole roll to head, drop to the thigh, to upper foot and let the ball fall to the ground. See Juggling Skills Nos. 1 and 19; Basic Control Techniques: *The Thigh Bounce* (Mario Tardelli); *The Top Foot Pace Absorber* (Socrates).

5 Perform a two-footed flick-up between heels, bringing the ball over the head and executing the bent volley with the inside of the foot. See Juggling Skill No. 21: Shooting and Passing: *The Bent Volley (Inside Foot)* (Steve Coppell).

Michel Platini on the deck against Northern Ireland. Donaghy (3), Hamilton and Chris Nicholl surround him.

Alan Brazil of Spurs finds the ball difficult to get at as Terry Butcher of Ipswich protects it and George Burley comes up in support.

Advanced steps in skill development

The advanced units of skill development as contained in the following ten sequences follow the same pattern as the early steps in skill development on the previous pages. Once the reader has mastered the early steps he is ready to practise these advanced sequences. Once again they are graded in difficulty, and the player should work through them in order, gradually developing skill and confidence in his ball control.

1

1 Flick up from sole roll. See Juggling Skill No. 1.

2 Perform a two-footed juggle – five each foot. See Juggling Skill No. 4.

3 Perform a thigh juggle – two each thigh. See Juggling Skill No. 9.

4 Perform a top foot pace absorber. See Basic Control Techniques: *The Top Foot Pace Absorber* (Socrates).

5 Perform the sole roll technique over a 15-metre dribbling run. See Dribbling Skills: *The Cross Pull* (Zico), component four.

2

1 Perform the instep trap at the back of the standing foot from a thrown ball. See Basic Control Techniques: *The Instep Trap at the Back of the Standing Foot* (Kevin Keegan).

2 Perform one step-over over a 15-metre dribbling run. See Dribbling Skills: *The Step-over* (Eder).

3 Take a bent ground shot with the inside of the foot at a target. See Shooting and Passing: *The Bent Ground Shot (Outside Foot)* (Paulo Rossi).

4 From the rebound apply outside foot spin with the ball circling outside the player. See Basic Control Techniques: *Back Spin with the Ball Circling Outside Player* (Liam Brady).

5 Perform one pull and push over a 15-metre dribbling run. See Dribbling Skills: *The Pull and Push* (Diego Maradona).

3

1 From a thrown ball apply an instep trap at the back of the standing foot. Allow escape, bringing the ball round to the front of the standing foot.

2 Perform a one-footed mobile juggle over 15 metres. See Juggling Skill No. 15.

3 Perform a head juggle. Five touches. See Juggling Skill No. 19.

4 Perform a step-over and outside foot flick. See Dribbling Skills: *The Step-over and Outside Foot Flick* (Eder).

5 Perform a step-over and play with the outside of the other foot. See Dribbling Skills: *The Step-over and Play with the Outside of the Other Foot* (Kevin O'Callaghan).

4

1 From a thrown ball perform a juggle spin, moving backwards. See Juggling Skill No. 12.

2 From a thrown ball, perform a two-touch shoulder juggle. See Juggling Skill No. 15.

3 Perform a cross-legged outside foot trap. See Basic Control Techniques: *The Cross-legged Outside Foot Trap* (Ray Wilkins).

4 Perform a flick-up and catch trap. See Juggling Skill No. 1; Basic Control Techniques: *The Top Foot Catch* (Ramon Diaz).

5 Kick the ball over the head and use top foot pace absorber. See Basic Control Techniques: *The Top Foot Pace Absorber* (Socrates).

5

1 Kick the ball, using the back of the standing foot technique. See Shooting and Passing: *Shot or Pass from behind the Standing Foot* (Gordon Cowans).

2 Perform a step-over and ride. See Dribbling Skills: *The Step-over and Ride* (Kenny Dalglish).

3 Chip the ball for the upper foot and thigh combination juggle. See Juggling Skill No. 10.

4 Perform one touch, both shoulders and head juggle. See See Juggling Skill No. 20.

5 Swerve the half-volley (outside foot) at a target from 25 metres. See Shooting and Passing: *Swerving the Half-volley (Outside Foot)* (Bernd Schuster).

6

1 From a thrown ball, use the top-foot scissors trap with the ball going through the legs. See Basic Control Techniques: *The Top Foot Pace Absorber (Scissor Movement) with Ball Taken Through Legs* (Alain Giresse).

2 Perform a 30-metre dribbling run using both outside foot surfaces. See Dribbling Skills: *Dribbling Using Both Outside Foot Surfaces* (Mark Barham).

3 Perform a two-footed pincer flick. See Juggling Skill No. 2.

4 Using both feet and both thighs perform a mobile juggle over 20 metres. See Juggling Skills Nos. 16 and 17.

5 Perform a convex chest trap with the ball rolling down the body. See Basic Control Techniques: *The Convex Chest Trap with Ball Rolling Down Body* (Michel Platini).

7

1 Perform two reverse step-overs over 15 metres. See Dribbling Skills: *The Reverse Step-over* (Mark Chamberlain).

2 Perform a flick-up between heel and top-foot. See Juggling Skill No. 22.

3 Perform a thigh bounce and top foot catch. See Basic Control Techniques: *The Thigh Bounce* (Marco Tardelli); *The Top Foot Catch* (Ramon Diaz).

4 Perform a top foot catch and carry. See Juggling Skill No. 7.

5 Perform top foot control over 15 metres pulling the ball through at four different angles. See Dribbling Skills: *Sole of the Foot Control* (Paul Mariner).

8

1 Receive a ball played along the ground and perform the swivel turn. See Dribbling Skills: *Pass Received and Swivel Turn* (Trevor Francis).

2 Perform a flick-up between heel and toe bringing the ball over the player's head. See Juggling Skill No. 22.

3 Perform three consecutive shoulder shots against a wall or from a thrown ball. See Shooting and Passing: *The Shoulder Shot or Pass* (Norman Whiteside).

4 Perform an upper foot, thigh and head mobile juggle over 20 metres. See Juggling Skills Nos 10 and 19.

5 Repeat, running backwards. See Juggling Skills as above.

9

1 Perform the step-over. See Dribbling Skills: *The Step-over* (Eder).

2 Repeat the step-over with back foot drag. See Dribbling Skills: *The Step-over with Back Foot Drag* (Eder).

3 Perform the swivel. See Dribbling Skills: *The Swivel* (Trevor Francis).

4 Perform a pull and push. See Dribbling Skills: *The Pull and Push* (Diego Maradona).

5 Perform a cross pull. See Dribbling Skills: *The Cross Pull* (Zico).

10

1 Perform the inside foot flick from passed ball. See Basic Control Technique: *The Inside Foot Flick* (George Best).

2 Perform the swivel through legs and turn. See Dribbling Skills: *The Ball Through Legs and Swivel* (Trevor Francis).

3 Perform a flick-up to head to neck trap and back to the head. See Juggling Skill No. 23.

4 Perform a top foot catch trap. Three catches each foot. See Juggling Skill No. 6.

5 Run beneath the ball and use heel shot. See Shooting and Passing: *Heel Shot or Pass after Running beneath the Ball* (Falcao).

Trevor Brooking in the colours of his only club, West Ham United.

Skill Practice Games

The games in this section have been devised to provide fun and a competitive or co-operative element in training.

Some can be played by two players, others are games for squad training. They are not to be regarded as substitutes for practising the skills in the previous sections. Nor are they meant as lighthearted breaks in training. Their virtue is that they provide variety in training sessions, they encourage camaraderie and team-spirit among colleagues and, of course, all the time a player is kicking, heading, running, and anticipating he is improving his basic control of the ball.

Head Tennis

1 The court to be agreed by the players.

2 The number of players to be agreed. The size of the court should be taken into account when deciding on numbers.

3 The net should be two metres from the ground.

4 The ball can be served with the head from a forward section of the court or with a kick from the base line.

5 The number of bounces permitted should be agreed between the players and the ability of the players should be taken into account when deciding this.

6 Only one player may touch the ball with surfaces other than the head, after which the ball must be played with the head.

7 The ball can be played with the head between players in their own court a predetermined number of times (e.g. three)

8 A point can only be awarded to the serving team.

9 A team continues to serve until it fails to win the point.

Foot Tennis

1 The court should be stipulated by the coach or in his absence agreed between the players. Badminton, volley ball or basketball courts all have suitable dimensions.

2 The number of players to be agreed, though between four and six per side is a suitable number.

3 The net should be about one and a quarter metres high.

4 Service is taken from the base line with a volley from a bounced ball.

5 The ball can be returned by any surface other than the hands.

6 For good players the game is more exciting if only one bounce is permitted. The number of bounces allowed should be determined by the overall ability of the players involved.

7 Each player may touch the ball only once before it is returned over the net.

8 A point can only be awarded to the serving team.

9 A team continues to serve until it fails to win the point.

All-Touch Tennis

1 The court and net height are the same as that used for Head Tennis.

2 A maximum of four players is recommended for this game.

3 The ball can be served with the head from a forward section of the court or with a kick from the base line.

4 Good players can play off one bounce while average players may need two or even three bounces.

5 When the ball has crossed the net every player in the side must touch the ball before it is returned.

6 All surfaces except the hands are allowed.

7 A point can only be awarded to the serving team.

8 A team continues to serve until it fails to win the point.

Hit and Run

1 The court dimensions are the same as for Head Tennis. There should be two lines, one one each side of the net, dividing the front court from the back court. The back court will consistute one-third of the playing surface on each side of the net.

2 The rules are the same as for Head Tennis except for the changes described in the next two rules.

3 The net should be one metre off the ground.

4 When a ball is played from a back court zone the player who played the ball must follow the ball, jumping the net, and may try to stop his opponents playing the ball back. This includes the service which makes running automatic from the kick. Running does not take place when a ball is played from the front court.

5 No physical contact is allowed and the use of the hands is barred. Feet must not be raised above the knee level in an attempt to block a return.

6 When a player returns to his own court he must do so along one side of the playing area.

7 Teams should concentrate on getting players into back court zones and on playing high balls which give the runner more time to get into the opposing court.

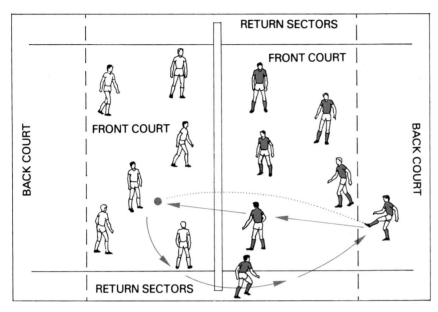

Soccer Squash

1 The court has to be agreed by the players concerned as does the wall surface. A suggested plan is shown on this page.

2 The number of bounces allowed before return should be agreed before the game and the ability of both players should be taken into account when deciding this.

3 The ball should be served from behind the agreed serving line from a dropped volley kick.

4 The ball can be returned without waiting for the bounces.

5 The ball can be juggled up to three times before it is played.

6 The ball must bounce inside the agreed boundaries.

7 When the ball is obviously going out of court but is played by an opponent and subsequently goes out this counts against the player who last played the ball.

8 Points are awarded regardless of service, which alternates.

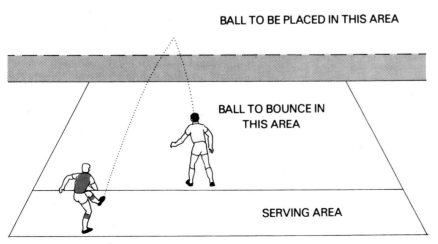

Target Squash

1 The dimensions and rules for this game are the same as for Soccer Squash except that three circles are drawn on the wall.

2 The centre one should have a diameter of half a metre while the outside ones should be one metre. A circle of one metre diameter should

be placed on the floor two metres from the wall and central to the outer boundaries. The players should concentrate on hitting these targets, which earn them bonus points.

3 If a player kicks a ball inside the centre circle he scores three bonus points. If he kicks it inside the two outer circles he scores two bonus points.

4 If he hits the centre circle on the wall and the ball on its first bounce falls in the circle on the ground he automatically wins the game.

5 Points are awarded regardless of service, which alternates.

6 Where targets are missed the game continues to be scored in the normal way.

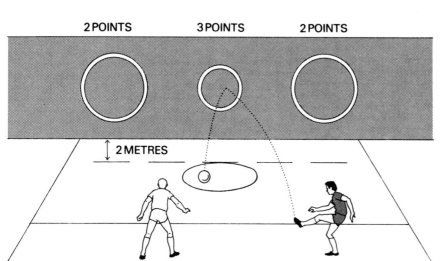

2 POINTS 3 POINTS 2 POINTS

2 METRES

Bench Football

1 Two teams should be selected. There should not be more than six in each.

2 They are placed in diagonally opposite corners of the hall or pitch (see diagram).

3 The pitch should be about the size of a usual five-a-side pitch.

4 A bench is placed on its side with

the seats facing into the pitch two yards in from each by-line.

5 The ball is placed in the centre of the pitch.

6 Each player on both sides is given a number from one to six.

7 The referee shouts a number and the player with that number sprints round the outside of the pitch past

his opponents' goal until he gets round to his own goal. He jumps over the centre of the bench and sprints for the ball. The other player will have jumped over the bench at the other end of the pitch.

8 The two players then try to score a goal by hitting their opponents' bench. The pitch should be divided into quarters. To score, a player must pass into the last quarter of the pitch. This is to encourage the player to dribble and retain possession, as well as to vary the pace. Where shooting practice is required this rule can be waived.

9 The referee can call more than one number. He may, at the end of the activity, call six numbers.

10 When two players have failed to score over a long period, and fatigue has set in, the referee can call reinforcements.

11 Where the coach wants to condition a game by creating three against one or three against four situations he may point to the end when he calls a number. He must first point to the end which is to be in the minority.

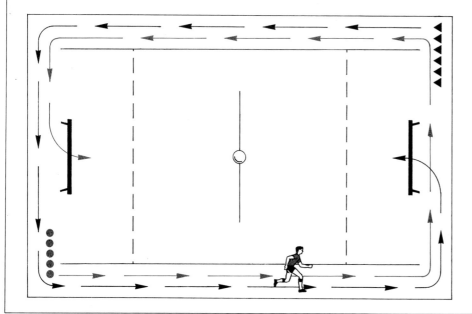

Driving Lessons

1 The players stand five metres apart facing each other.

2 The player with the ball passes it to his partner who returns it.

3 The second player then moves backwards and continues to move backwards while the ball is passed between himself and his partner, who is moving forwards.

4 When the player who is running forwards changes his angle subsequent movement goes in a straight line from this point.

5 The object is for the player running backwards to reach a predetermined target in a given time.

6 As running backwards is more tiring than running forwards, roles should be reversed from time to time.

7 A competitive element can be added by attempting to beat the record time.

Flying Lessons

1 The two partners face each other about five metres apart.

2 One player holds the ball.

3 He lobs the ball to his partner who can return it using any surface other than the hands.

4 Having returned it, the player starts to move backwards.

5 Moving in this way, the two players keep the ball in the air trying to reach a predetermined target.

6 As with Driving Lessons, a competitive element can be introduced by trying to beat the record time.

A Juggle Swop

1 Both players stand in their own circle which should have a diameter of at least five metres.

2 The two circles should be four metres apart.

3 One player juggles with the ball until he has absolute control.

4 He then calls his partner's name and plays the ball vertically into the air.

5 The partner has to sprint to the other circle and endeavour to catch the ball before it hits the ground.

6 The partner who played the ball into the air has meanwhile sprinted to the other circle where he waits.

7 It is now the turn of the player who has controlled the ball to call his partner and play the ball into the air.

8 This is a partnership game, the two players helping each other.

9 Scores should be kept of the number of successful rallies.

10 Efforts should be made to beat the existing record score.

5 METRES DIAMETER

4 METRES

Wall Head-ball

1 Both players stand facing a high wall.

2 The first player throws the ball high against the wall.

3 The second player then heads the ball back against the wall.

4 Taking turns the two players try to keep the ball going between themselves and the wall.

5 This is another partnership game, the players helping each other and keeping score of the headers made before the ball touches the ground.

6 A competitive element is added by attempting to beat the record score.

Wall Juggle

1 This is a game for two players, who play as a team rather than against each other.

2 The ball is played against the wall by one player from a bounce.

3 Once it has hit the wall it should be controlled by the other player and played back against the wall without touching the ground.

4 Each player is allowed two touches to control the ball before returning it to the wall.

5 Keep count of the strikes against the wall without the ball touching the ground.

6 This is essentially a co-operative and not a competitive exercise. The aim should be to produce situations which make it easier for your partner rather than difficult.

7 The object of each pair should be to beat the record score of the day.

Photographic Acknowledgements

The colour and black and white photographs featured in this book were provided by the following sources :
Associated Sports Photography: George Herringshaw
Colour Library International

Colorsport
David Spurdens

Sequences photographed by David Spurdens

GREENWICH LIBRARIES